The Charity First series aims to provide practical and straightforward guidance on the challenges confronting charity operations today, with fundraising in the spotlight. Its individual subjects range from those concentrating on the UK and Ireland to non-profit issues in the EU and other jurisdictions, from traditional to digital fundraising and from basic help for those just entering the third sector to specialist areas for the more experienced.

For further information and orders see www.charityfirstseries.org

RAISING FUNDS FOR YOUR SCHOOL
A comprehensive guide

Nick Ryan

First published in Great Britain 2017 by
Social Partnership Marketing LLP
38 Leconfield Road, London N5 2SN

© Nick Ryan, 2017

A CIP catalogue record for this book is available from the British Library.

ISBN: 978-1-908595-36-2

Printed in Great Britain by CPI Group (UK) Ltd, Croydon, CR0 4YY.

Limit of Liability/Disclaimer. While the publisher and author have used their best efforts in preparing this publication, they make no representations or warranties in respect of the accuracy or completeness of the contents of this publication. If legal advice or other expert assistance is required, the services of a competent professional should be sought.

Raising Funds for Your School is a title in The Charity First Series: www.charityfirstseries.org.

We acknowledge with gratitude the assistance of The Southern Co-operative towards the production of this book.

To Meg, Ben and Lucy, for keeping me grounded.

CONTENTS

Foreword . v

1
Introduction . 1

2
The basics - how much should we take on? . 3

3
Who does what and where do I fit in? . 7
Head teacher . 7
Parents . 8
Governors . 8
School business manager / Bursar . 9
Staff . 9
Pupils . 9
Alumni . 10
Professional fundraisers . 10

4
What type of support do we want? . 13
Cash . 13
Volunteers . 15
In-kind support . 16

5
What are we going to do to raise the money? . 19
Fundraising activities . 19
Prioritising your activities – complexity and effort . 25

6
Reaching out - who is going to support us? . 27
Ethical considerations . 27
Potential donors you might approach . 29
Donor motivations . 31

7
Making the approach . 36
Blanket approach versus personalised approach . 36
Type of approach . 37
Determining who will make the approach . 39

Timing your approaches . 41
Bringing everything together . 41

8
The fundraising disciplines . 45

Newsletter . 45
Website . 49
Community fundraising . 51
Event fundraising . 53
Trust and statutory applications . 56
Raffles and lotteries . 60
Recycling as a fundraiser . 62
Payroll Giving . 63
Major donor fundraising . 65
Company fundraising . 73
Exploiting school premises . 76
Sponsorship . 77
Text giving . 79
Legacies . 80
Cause related marketing . 83

9
The Case for Support . 88

Essential content . 88
A comprehensive document . 89
A work in progress . 90

10
Fundraising tools to give you an edge . 92

Gift Aid . 92
30-second pitch . 93
Match-giving . 94
Crowdfunding . 96
Listening and questioning . 97
Social media overview . 97
Facebook . 100
Twitter . 103
Stand-out features . 104
Storytelling . 106
Networking . 107
Psychology of influence . 109

11
Dealing with rejections . 113

12
Overcoming donor apathy and stalling . 116
Restarting stalled funding requests . 116
Engaging non-participants . 119

13
Someone has given! . 123
Recognition tables . 123
Recognition and donor motivations . 123
Shrinking violets . 124
It's too good to be true! . 124

14
Keeping donors happy . 126
Who goes into the Stewardship Programme? . 126
Databases . 126
Activities to keep your donors engaged . 126
Segmentation (personalisation) . 128
End-of-year reports . 128
Being contactable . 129
Expanding your workforce . 129

15
Campaigns - bringing it all together . 132
Annual Campaigns . 132
Capital Campaigns . 138
Endowments . 143

16
Summary . 146

17
Resources . 147
Directories of funders . 147
Other fundraising resources . 148
Bibliography . 150

About the author . 153

Index . 155

LIST OF TABLES

Table No	Title	Page
1	Determining which project to support	14
2	Timetable of activities	42
3	Major donor prospect list	43
4	Head teacher prospect list	43
5	Prioritised prospect list	69
6	Recognition table	123
7	A gift table for a £50,000 campaign	134
8	Testing the effectiveness of two mailings	136
9	Annual Campaign effectiveness: income	137
10	Annual Campaign effectiveness: donor numbers	137
11	Annual Campaign effectiveness: gift sizes	138

FOREWORD

As a funder of schools and educational projects in London since the mid eighteenth century, Sir John Cass's Foundation is keenly aware of the constant financial demands faced by all who have a responsibility for educational provision. Though many facets of the educational sector will evolve and change over time, some features remain constant, and among these the need to maintain the highest educational standards and to offer the broadest range of opportunities for the enrichment of all our young people are always of paramount importance. At the best of times these requirements place heavy demands on school heads and managers, but in times of financial constraint – such as when public funding is frozen or in decline - the challenge of how to provide sound, broad-based education in the sort of well-equipped school environments that are most conducive to personal development and learning becomes particularly acute. This is a stark challenge facing many schools at present, at all age levels from primary through to further education.

To meet this funding challenge, all schools are likely in future to need to learn how to attract voluntary income, to complement funds received from public and other sources. The higher education sector has demonstrated in recent years that this is an eminently achievable ambition, though the majority of schools currently lag some way behind, as they lack both the information on how to develop a fundraising strategy, and the culture that can help fundraising programmes to take root and thrive.

In Raising Funds for Your School, Nick Ryan addresses both of these requirements. Whilst providing clear non-technical advice to help heads, teachers, schools administrators and parents' groups alike to develop fundraising activities, he gives especial consideration to how to embed such activities into the life of the school, increasing their salience, their joint ownership and their chance of success.

We first worked with Nick more than a decade ago when he headed up the fundraising division at the Specialist Schools and Academies Trust. From the outset, it was clear that this was someone who knew his subject matter and was determined to advance the sector. This was a key reason why we channelled approximately £1 million into the Specialist Schools Programme. Indeed, it was particularly interesting to read the section in this book on match-funding as our 7-figure donation unlocked an 8-figure one from Government.

More recently we worked with Nick, along with other founding partners such as *The Guardian* and Baroness Walmsley, to set up Schools Funding Network. This initiative takes away a lot of the complexity found in everyday fundraising, such as Gift Aid. However, there is still no hiding away from the fact that there needs to be a significant uplift in knowledge and skills within primary and secondary education if funding potential is to be realised; it already happens in the United States so we know it can be done here. This book will provide readers with the information needed to raise those transformational amounts of funding. Indeed, it covers all elements necessary for a school to create a complete fundraising strategy. While broad-ranging and detailed in its coverage of fundraising methods, its easy, non-technical approach will make it an accessible and stimulating manual even for those entirely new to this field. I commend it warmly to all schools.

Richard Foley
Clerk and Chief Executive
Sir John Cass's Foundation, The Education Charity for London
sirjohncassfoundation.com

1
INTRODUCTION

The first decade of the 21st century brought increases in school budgets and there was much investment in education. That is no longer the case. As a result, the latest generation of school children risk facing a slimmed down educational offer. For instance, a recent survey of school governors for the *Times Educational Supplement* found that:

- 1 in 3 schools said that financial constraints had led to the school's offer to pupils being reduced
- 60% of schools said that they would need to reduce spending on staff over the next 2 years
- 40% of schools had cut staff in the last year
- 30% of schools reduced the number of subjects on offer to pupils.

Yet, there are means of making up such a shortfall. Fundraising is one such way.

While the need to raise funds may appear as an additional chore, this book shows that well-planned fundraising can offer many benefits to the school. The most obvious is an increased revenue stream, which can be extremely significant when fundraising is done at scale. However, fundraising can bring an array of other advantages, such as expert advice, new contacts and political influence. By developing your fundraising, you will also help to integrate the school more closely with its community and increase general engagement levels. Indeed, you will almost certainly be surprised at all the opportunities that come your way.

Raising Funds for Your School is designed as a manual to help schools, no matter what level of fundraising they are engaged in or how much past experience they may have. In the introductory chapters (2-4) we look at the preliminary requirements for establishing a successful programme – assessment of the available resources, establishment of a fundraising 'culture' and agreement on priority needs – followed, in Chapter 5, by a brief overview of the different options for raising support. Chapter 6 then looks at different sources of funding available and the ways in which they can be accessed followed, in Chapter 7, by a discussion of the mechanics of making approaches to funders – and how, when and by whom they should be made. Chapter 8 looks at fundraising from a different angle, serving as a 'how to' compendium of the various fundraising opportunities and methods first described in Chapter 5. Some users may like to treat this central section as a stand-alone manual.

Chapter 9 looks in detail at how to create a Case for Support, which is the key fundraising document in any serious fundraising campaign, and Chapter 10 lists ways in which fundraising can be 'tweaked' to yield even better results. Chapters 11 and 12 then consider the management of fundraising when things don't go quite to plan, and chapters 13 and 14 look at the cultivation of donors to establish strong long-term relationships. Finally, in Chapter 15, drawing on the advice given in earlier chapters, the advanced fundraising techniques required to run Annual, Capital and Endowment Fund Campaigns are described. The book is completed by a Resources section signposting useful websites and literature.

To get the most from the book, it is recommended that you first skim-read it. This will give you a helpful overview of what can be achieved. It would then be worth focusing on one or two fundraising disciplines, either improving existing work that you are doing or developing new strands. Any more than that and you risk being swamped. Of course, once you have integrated a new fundraising stream then focus on another.

Another important point is to avoid thinking that you need to completely master all the information before you begin. Yes, being completely at ease with the techniques will undoubtedly help you but you are only likely to reach that point by putting the advice into action. So much better to reach out to donors and prospects and learn from your mistakes, using the book as a guide to dip in and out of. After all, every fundraiser is a human being and none of us is perfect!

While fundraising can certainly be stressful, particularly if you have demanding targets, it can also be great fun. Hopefully, this book will give you the knowledge to be sure that you are doing the right thing and the confidence to be yourself when talking with funders.

2
THE BASICS - HOW MUCH SHOULD WE TAKE ON?

Before diving straight into your fundraising, it is worth working out what might and might not be feasible in your school.

To determine what you should be doing, consider these aspects:

- Capacity
- Expertise
- Employees versus volunteers
- History of giving
- Ability to increase capacity
- Strategic need

i. Capacity

If you are a teacher who has fundraising tagged on to the main job or are just a couple of keen parents with little or no extra support then you will find it demoralising, and indeed pointless, to undertake all of the techniques and processes described in this book. On the other hand, if you have a variety of people willing to help then a range of fundraising activities becomes possible.

Where you do have many helpers, consider how they are deployed. It is much better for people to specialise so you can undertake a number of fundraising activities rather than focusing on just one. For instance, asking one or two volunteers to write funding applications rather than helping with another event should soon pay dividends.

Chapter 8 explains how the individual fundraising techniques work in practice; this background is worth reading thoroughly before taking on a new area.

ii. Expertise

If you are new to a particular fundraising technique then it will take time to get up to speed. For instance, if you have never undertaken corporate fundraising and only do event fundraising then you will probably be better advised looking at other, simpler activities before approaching companies. The section Prioritising your activities – complexity and effort (Page 25) provides a list of fundraising activities rated by ease and simplicity which will help you determine where to focus your attention.

iii. Employees versus volunteers

Generally, it is better for volunteers to work on the less technically demanding aspects of fundraising, such as events, and paid staff to focus on aspects like application-writing and meeting major donors. One reason for this is that volunteers often need to see immediate returns and, however good or bad an event, money is likely to come in.

On the other hand, dealing with major donors does not always culminate in support, can result in detailed questions and takes time. These are things which can put off volunteers and, even if they are willing to do such things, it could take two to three years to cultivate a major gift, by which time the volunteer has moved on.

iv. History of giving

If you have a history of at least one major donor giving regularly to your school then you should probably aim to have somebody with major donor fundraising skills available somewhere in your school. For instance, if a company gives you significant support every year then you know that there is something about your school that is attractive to companies (assuming that the company head is not married to the head teacher!). Consequently, in these situations, where you have nobody skilled in corporate fundraising, it would be worthwhile training someone up or bringing in outside help.

v. Ability to increase capacity

If, having read the above, you find yourself limited in the amount of fundraising you can undertake then you might be able to change this by:

- Recruiting more volunteers
- Increasing the amount of time spent on fundraising by staff
- Bringing in outside support, such as a consultant
- Undertaking training
- Involving pupils
- Reading this book!

vi. Strategic need

Sometimes fundraising is the only option available to you. If you need a new building or want to create first-class facilities then a carefully planned and executed fundraising drive might well be the only route. Employing a consultant is one way that you can speed up your fundraising journey, particularly if they are well-connected. Training is also an option but be realistic – it takes time to embed the techniques. Finally, if you must develop a significant new fundraising stream, be aware that fundraising usually incurs a cost at the start before income comes in.

2. The basics - how much should we take on?

Chapter 2 in a nutshell

Every school has a unique set of people and circumstances. That means that there is no one-size-fits-all solution for maximising your fundraising income. Not every school will be able to undertake every fundraising activity, while some schools will have a surfeit of opportunities.

It is therefore recommended that fundraising planning should begin with a practical assessment of what can be achieved in view of the complexity of different techniques, on the one hand, and the available human resources, on the other. Where there is a pressing need to raise significant sums, specialist external assistance may be required.

3
WHO DOES WHAT AND WHERE DO I FIT IN?

A successful school fundraising operation will not be undertaken in isolation. Rather it will involve a variety of different people and groups working towards a common goal. Having said that, each will have different motivations and the challenge is to meet these.

The list below showcases the key groups that should be engaged, with details of their motivations. The latter is important because not everyone sees the importance of fundraising and it is a rare school indeed that has everyone aligned behind the discipline. For instance, a head teacher might see raising support as a distraction from a purely pedagogical focus, while parents might be disengaged as a result of having previous efforts go largely unrecognised. Consequently, tips for bringing the various stakeholders onside have been included.

Head teacher
Types of activity
- Meeting and greeting prospects
- Thanking donors
- Explaining the importance of projects to stakeholders
- Adding gravitas to a campaign

Motivation
Well-being of children, Ofsted outcomes, exam results, comparison with neighbouring schools

Overcoming engagement difficulties
- Stress parents' and donors' expectations that the head teacher be engaged
- Compare with other head teachers who are engaged successfully with fundraising
- Limit involvement to the most important occasions
- Seek VIP donors to bring to the school to meet the head
- Emphasise the impact successful fundraising outcomes will have on educational outcomes

Parents
Types of activity
- Run events
- Write applications
- Source money and items
- Oversee recycling initiatives

Motivation
Support of their children; participation in the school community; social engagement with other parents; gaining the esteem of the head teacher and others; contribution to the ethos of the school; setting an example to their children

Overcoming engagement difficulties
- Stress impact on their children's lives
- Ask one parent to explain the benefits of fundraising
- Explain the need in simple language where English is limited (even translate if necessary)
- Have the head teacher or deputy head give a talk explaining the need for fundraising

Governors
Types of activity
- Meet prospects
- Introduce prospects to the school
- Write proposals
- Source information

Motivation
Well-being of children, Ofsted outcomes, exam results, comparison with neighbouring schools

Overcoming engagement difficulties
- Set minimum giving level for governors (this weeds out those not fully engaged)
- Benchmark with schools slightly ahead of yours in fundraising
- Demonstrate how fundraising can help with governors' pet projects
- Show how fundraising can improve parents' perceptions
- Show how fundraising can help with Ofsted inspections

School business manager / Bursar
Types of activity
- Explain tax benefits to major donors
- Negotiate commercial partnerships
- Claim and operate Gift Aid
- Plan and oversee Campaigns
- Meet donors interested in the business rather than the emotional side of giving

Motivation
Financial health of organisation; head teacher's approval

Overcoming engagement difficulties
- Ensure that any additional work is kept to a minimum (often they are very busy)
- Show how fundraising can help overcome budgetary weaknesses
- Ask head teacher for support

Staff
Types of activity
- Write a vision for their departments to be presented to donors
- Provide quotes and a direct link to the children, these being the beneficiaries most donors want to help, rather than schools per se
- Provide a list of desired items, large and small
- Meet with donors
- Facilitate events

Motivation
Improved results within their own departments; increased involvement with the school as a whole; acquisition of new skills; enhanced CVs

Overcoming engagement difficulties
- Stress impact on results, particularly their own subject areas
- Emphasise additional equipment and resource that will be given to the particular department

Pupils
Types of activity
- Meet and greet donors

- Fundraise themselves
- Perform at events
- Help organise events
- Provide quotes, thank-you notes and updates to those who support

Motivation
Developing CVs; acquiring non-academic skills; displaying skills (e.g. musical ones at an fundraising soirée); for advocates of an old-fashioned approach: simple obligation!

Overcoming engagement difficulties
- Explain impact on future job and university applications
- Ask older pupils to explain benefits to younger people
- Stress the fun elements of fundraising

Alumni
Types of activity
- Give career talks
- Run alumni events
- Bring on other alumni
- Link their companies to your school

Motivation
Demonstration of personal success; recollection of fond memories of their school days; desire to help children brought up in the same area as themselves; desire to improve the neighbourhood

Overcoming engagement difficulties
- Strengthen relationships with alumni, for instance increase number of communications such as newsletters
- Showcase what other alumni are doing
- Invite old pupils to the school

Professional fundraisers[1]
Types of activity
- Write proposals and letters on behalf of others

---

[1] Any school employing a professional fundraiser is now required by law to enter into a written agreement, signed by both parties, which specifies the terms and objectives of the arrangement. See www.fundraisingregulator.org.uk/l8-0-professional-fundraisers-agreements/ for further details.

- Write large bids
- Facilitate major donor meetings
- Co-ordinate major donor events
- Advise on tax and other matters
- Be the 'go-to' expert for the school's non-professional fundraisers
- Run Campaigns
- Open doors to funders inaccessible to you

Motivation

Development of the school; surpassing professional fundraising benchmarks; gaining respect within the school

Overcoming engagement difficulties
- Set milestones
- Give a bonus for over-performance[2]
- Find a replacement!

---

[2] Be very wary of professional fundraisers offering to work for you on a commission basis and do not offer this as a shortcut to save upfront expenditure. Not only does commission create conflicts of interest but funders themselves dislike such arrangements immensely i.e. you will severely curtail your fundraising potential.

3. Who does what and where do I fit in?

Chapter 3 in a nutshell

For fundraising to be most effective, a key preliminary requirement is for a fundraising 'culture' to be developed, with the collective involvement of as many different stakeholders in the life of the school as possible.

Determining the motivation of the individual elements of your fundraising team is a key first step in engagement. Tips are given for bringing different stakeholders onside.

4
WHAT TYPE OF SUPPORT DO WE WANT?

While virtually anything that might be of use to your school could be appealed for, the kinds of support available fall under three main categories:

- Cash
- Volunteers
- In-kind support

Cash

Cash is usually the priority when fundraising and will undoubtedly be a key driver in most schools' activities.

i. Choosing your project(s)

The first step when fundraising is to determine which project or projects to focus your attention on. After all, there will be numerous projects which are worthy of additional support. So how do you determine on which to spend time fundraising? Answering the following questions will help you decide:

- How much of a difference will it make to the school as a whole?
- How attractive will it be to potential funders?
- How much funding is required as a percentage of the school's largest successful fundraising request?

Example: You send an email to all staff in your school saying that you are looking for projects for which to fundraise. You receive three suggestions:

> Project A – A minibus to take pupils to external events and activities: cost £15,000
> Project B – A trip to fly three pupils to the UN Headquarters in America: cost £5,000
> Project C – A new building on some spare land: cost £150,000

You then fill in the table below, grading each cell on a scale from 1 to 10. This makes clear that Project A is the one to choose.

4. What type of support do we want?

	A	B	C
Difference to school as a whole	7	3	8
Attractiveness to funders	8	3	10
Funding required in relation to previous efforts	6	9	1
Total	**21**	**15**	**19**

Table 1 Determining which project to support

The advantage of having such a methodology is that it overcomes a common mistake whereby the project which someone, usually the head teacher, is most passionate about is put forward. This can lead to plenty of frustration and wasted effort - external donors fail to materialise or you vainly attempt to fit your project into funders' criteria only to see your applications thrown out as not fitting the briefs.

ii. Overcoming resistance

Invariably, someone will object to your project choice. If this is a subject head then you can often assuage them by pointing out why a different area was taken up, allowing them the opportunity to modify their future requests. However, if it is the head teacher who is insistent on an inappropriate project then you have more of an issue.

Means of tackling this include:

- Asking an influential donor to explain why your favoured project is better.
- Listing all the donors who you think would support your favoured project compared with the other.
- Feeding back comments from failed approaches if you have to adopt the unattractive project.

iii. Case for Support

The Case for Support, as we will see later, is an important document which provides all the information needed to raise funds successfully for an organisation. Any projects which have been written up should be included in this overarching document. In this way, anybody approaching a funder has the requisite knowledge to put forward the school's aims and needs, including budgetary details.

Volunteers

Attracting volunteers might not seem obviously related to fundraising, but in fact volunteers can be as, and indeed more, beneficial than cash. Indeed, certain funders, such as companies, may initially be more willing to provide volunteering support than to offer cash. Fortunately, the skills required to attract and retain volunteers – particularly the ability to motivate and enthuse - are largely the same as those needed to raise cash.

i. Attracting volunteers

A national survey on volunteering[3] found that:

- 60% say lack of time is why they don't volunteer
- 40% say lack of time is why they stop volunteering

And yet 15 million people say they want to volunteer more! Given the potential uplift in volunteering numbers, here are a few approaches for attracting more volunteers:

- **Better understand the time obstacles people face**
  Despite all our labour-saving devices, we are busier than ever. As a result, you need to give thought as to how potential volunteers might interact with you – they will not all be the same. For instance, if all of your volunteering opportunities take place during the working day, you effectively exclude working parents and anybody else busy at that time. Try to accommodate different lifestyles so that you benefit from as wide a group of people as possible.

- **Break up roles into bite-sized chunks**
  Being able to help out once a term in some capacity is likely to be something that more people feel they can commit to, rather than longer-term projects, such as being a school governor. Similarly, activities which can be undertaken during the evening or at weekends will broaden your volunteering appeal.

- **Allow people to dip in and out**
  One fear that volunteers have is that they will let their school down if they need to pull out unexpectedly. As a result, they do not

---

[3] Helping Out: A national survey of volunteering and charitable giving (Cabinet Office, 2007).

volunteer. While you do not want to remove all sense of duty, removing this fear will increase your volunteer numbers. Creating contingencies, such as having more than one volunteer covering a role, will ensure that you are not left in the lurch when somebody does drop out.

- **Be creative about what volunteers can do for you**
  The RSPB greatly increased the number of volunteers at its disposal by creating a volunteering activity that could be done in the volunteer's home; the Big Garden Birdwatch asks volunteers to spend just one hour counting the birds in their garden. Being similarly creative could bring in more volunteers and more support.

ii. Managing volunteers

Once you have attracted volunteers into the school, make sure that you induct, train and manage them effectively. It is surprising how many volunteers end up disillusioned with the commitment because they feel under-appreciated or are not really sure what they are doing.

To help engage volunteers, produce materials for each volunteering activity (this need not be expensive or time-consuming to produce) and periodically check how supported your volunteers feel. A timely thank you from the head teacher can be highly effective in re-energising such supporters.

In-kind support

In-kind support is often seen as the poor man in comparison to cash and volunteers. For instance, a lot of schools and charities will prefer to take cash and buy a piece of equipment, rather than simply receive the equipment in the first place. Yet there is little logical reason for this. Indeed, if you are willing and open to this kind of funding, you can receive a remarkable amount of support.

i. Why do funders give in-kind support?

Many funders, particularly companies, much prefer this form of giving. One reason for this preference is that in-kind support can be a lot cheaper to give in comparison to cash donations. For instance, if a company has surplus stock or is testing a new model, then an in-kind donation is an attractive way of giving, not least because it removes the need for salesmen or retail outlets.

4. What type of support do we want?

Another reason for this type of giving is to test the relationship with a school. By seeing how you work, how you receive the support, as well as give thanks, a funder can decide whether they want to become more involved. So, for such funders, this is a relatively risk-free way of supporting you initially.

ii. Asking for in-kind support
When talking to funders, make sure that you explore in-kind support. A lot of funders won't consider it, assuming that fundraising means cash support. So if you're talking to an office supplier, ask for office supplies. If you're talking to a lawyer, ask for pro bono legal advice. If you're talking to a fundraiser, ask them to look at your proposals. You get the idea, I trust!

4. What type of support do we want?

Chapter 4 in a nutshell

Fundraising is a much broader discipline than simply raising cash. While money is often the priority, volunteers and in-kind support can also make a significant difference to your school.

When determining what support you are seeking (and willing to accept), try to be as open as possible at this stage. If you are too particular then your negotiations with funders will be limited.

Projects for which you are raising support should be listed in your Case for Support. This document will inform the fundraisers of your school in their approaches to prospects and donors.

5
WHAT ARE WE GOING TO DO TO RAISE THE MONEY?

In this chapter, we will run briefly through the different options you have for raising support and consider which are appropriate for your school. For further information on these options and how to deliver them, please see chapter 8.

Fundraising activities
i. Newsletter
A newsletter provides a simple and clear means of telling your supporters and prospects of past, current and future fundraising activity. It should be a staple of your fundraising arsenal.

- **Pros**

    Simple and cheap to run, newsletters provide an excellent foundation to build other fundraising activities.

- **Cons**

    Certain donors and prospects will simply not engage with newsletters. You will need to find alternative ways to interact with them instead.

ii. Website
Like the newsletter, the website should be a *sine qua non* of your fundraising armoury. If you don't have a fundraising section to your website, you are sending out a very strong message that your fundraising is little advanced. Who then will give you large sums?

- **Pros**

    Easily accessible, your website will often be the first port of call for those wishing to know what is happening at your school and how they can get involved.

- **Cons**

    A cheap or poorly produced website will put off certain donors, particularly larger ones. For instance, if the website looks amateurish then what confidence will a donor have that a donation will be well managed?

iii. Community fundraisers

Holding collecting buckets before and after school or running a cake sale involves community fundraisers. In addition, allowing people to raise funds for you via marathons, sponsored walks and cycles, or any other third-party activity is a good way of tapping into a fundraising technique already much embedded in the public's psyche.

- **Pros**
  Most schools will have plenty of people willing to act as community fundraisers. In addition, some of the biggest fundraising platforms, such as JustGiving, are increasingly set up for this type of fundraising.

- **Cons**
  For the amount of work involved, this form of fundraising, despite being very popular, offers a low return on investment. In addition, some people will never engage in this way.

iv. Event fundraising

From the school fete to an evening fundraiser, events provide a useful means of bringing donors and prospects together in an enjoyable setting.

- **Pros**
  Events do not require much technical know-how to run. As a result, they are a canny option when there are a lot of willing, but largely inexperienced, fundraisers to hand. In addition, events can serve a variety of non-fundraising purposes, such as bringing the school community together, raising publicity for a bigger campaign or generally raising awareness of needs.

- **Cons**
  Events are time-consuming activities and largely produce less return for the effort expended compared with many of the other activities.

v. Trust and statutory applications

There are numerous government and charitable funds to which you can apply. Historically, this form of fundraising provides the best return on investment.

5. What are we going to do to raise the money?

- **Pros**
  Amounts available can be very large. In addition, most application forms explain clearly what is needed, thereby simplifying the application process considerably.

- **Cons**
  The majority of applications fail because they do not meet the criteria of the funder. So there is clearly a difficulty for many people either in reading the requirements, or in explaining why their project fits! Without inside information, it can also be difficult to know how competitive a fund will be – some are barely worth applying to because there will be so many applicants.

vi. Raffles and lotteries
Selling tickets that allow buyers to win prizes is an ever-popular means of raising funds.

- **Pros**
  These are excellent ways to generate money and the chances are that you will already be running one in some shape or form. They are simple and readily understandable.

- **Cons**
  Despite their simplicity, raffles and lotteries do require time and effort.

vii. Recycling as a fundraiser
A variety of materials can be recycled in return for money and most schools undertake at least some form of recycling.

- **Pros**
  Given the number of households linked to a typical school, there will be plenty of materials which you are able to recycle. This is a simple fundraising technique, which virtually anyone can take part in – so good for involving the whole community!

- **Cons**
  You are unlikely to bring in huge sums of money this way. In addition, storing materials prior to collection may be cumbersome.

viii. Payroll Giving

Parents and any other members of your school community who work for organisations that operate PAYE as part of their payrolls can potentially give to your school in a tax-effective and extremely simple way.

- **Pros**

    This is a good way of gaining a steady stream of long-term income. Donors like it, not least because it is tax-efficient.

- **Cons**

    Some employers will not be willing to set up such schemes.

ix. Major donor fundraising

Major donors are those able to give support which could make a significant difference to your school. For present purposes, we will consider all major donors as being individuals, keeping companies and other donor types separate. What is 'significant' will vary from school to school, but as a very rough rule of thumb anyone giving £5,000 might be considered 'major'.

- **Pros**

    As their name suggests, major donors have the power to make a real, transformative, difference to your school.

- **Cons**

    Major donors need warming up before they give, so this is not the quickest of fundraising disciplines. Given that major donors are people, with all the diversity and complexity that brings, there is a definite art to major donor fundraising, which often only comes with experience.

x. Company fundraising (also known as corporate fundraising)

Companies provide schools with a range of support from cash through to staff support.

- **Pros**

    Local businesses are often keen to support schools in their area, as are branches of national companies. For the right project, companies will give significant support, while partnerships, once formed, are often long-lasting.

5. What are we going to do to raise the money?

- **Cons**
  Corporate fundraising is perhaps the most technical of the fundraising disciplines. To be successful, you will need to show how support of your school marries with the specific business goals of the companies you approach. As a result, you will need a good working knowledge of business dynamics. In addition, many companies give to schools because they believe the association will improve their image and generate goodwill in the community. Some people in your school community will object to this, believing that companies should be giving purely benevolently or not at all.

xi. Exploiting school premises
Schools increasingly make more use of their premises to raise money. From hiring out school halls and existing facilities through to mixed partnership schemes, there are various ways you can monetise your structure.

- **Pros**
  Potentially, very large sums of money can be made in this way. In addition, a number of companies are willing to undertake all the work, from marketing to caretaking, on your behalf. It need not therefore be a particularly onerous source of income. It is also worth noting that many projects funded by the Big Lottery Fund require the involvement of the local community and this is a good way to meet those requirements.

- **Cons**
  Certain people will be against the school diversifying in such a way. Some arrangements can be very technical, requiring a high degree of time and effort as well. There are risks associated with this area which you will need to manage.

xii. Sponsorship
Sponsorship is a commercial relationship that results in funding being given to your school in return for the sponsor being able to associate itself with something belonging to you. It is an area that some schools have exploited extremely effectively.

- **Pros**
  Schools have a variety of activities and materials that make strong

sponsorship vehicles. In addition, there are a good many sponsors who wish to link with schools.

- **Cons**
  Negotiating a fair and profitable sponsorship agreement can be difficult. Delivery of some of the benefits offered in return for sponsorship can be onerous. Some people have ethical issues with sponsorship, considering the school as 'selling its soul'.

xiii. Text giving

Enabling people to give to your school by text is likely to increase donations from certain members of your school community. It is still quite a rare form of fundraising in most schools.

- **Pros**
  Any means of making it easier to give to your school should be welcome. The service offered by Vodafone is completely free to both donor and charity.

- **Cons**
  This is still very much a niche area and is unlikely to make a huge difference to your fundraising.

xiv. Legacies

More than £2 billion a year is left to good causes, yet few schools seek to attract this form of giving and even fewer do it well.

- **Pros**
  This is potentially a very large income source for your school.

- **Cons**
  There is no immediate impact, so a long-term strategy is required. It is essential to approach this form of fundraising sensitively.

xv. Cause related marketing (challenge fundraising)

Cause related marketing (CRM) involves a funder giving a donation to a specified good cause every time a certain action takes place. For example, a local business might give a school fifty pounds every time a new customer is introduced.

5. What are we going to do to raise the money?

- **Pros**
  The technique appeals to funders motivated by the *mutual benefit* motivation (see donor motivations, page 31), in particular companies.

- **Cons**
  It can be time-consuming to negotiate such arrangements.

Prioritising your activities – complexity and effort

You should look to build up your fundraising piecemeal. As your fundraising knowledge and skill increases, you can introduce new elements to the point where you are fully maximising your income.

The list below details how you might develop a fundraising function if you were starting from scratch.

1. Newsletter
2. Website
3. Community fundraisers
4. Event fundraising
5. Trust and statutory applications
6. Raffles and lotteries
7. Recycling
8. Payroll Giving
9. Major donor fundraising[4]
10. Company fundraising[5]
11. Exploiting school premises (simple)[6]
12. Sponsorship
13. Text giving
14. Legacies
15. Exploiting school premises (complex)[7]
16. Cause related marketing

If you have an expert in a certain field then, of course, move that particular activity up the priority list. For example, if you have a property lawyer in your midst then exploiting your school premises could well become a priority.

---

[4] Consider moving up the list if you are aware of certain rich individuals in your midst.
[5] Consider moving up if your school is based close to a business district.
[6] For example, renting out a school hall.
[7] For example, partnering with a housing association and creating a mixed-use site.

5. What are we going to do to raise the money?

> **Chapter 5 in a nutshell**
>
> The chapter gives an overview of the different options for raising support for the school, outlining the pros and cons of each of the activities described. A typical school would do well to incorporate the fundraising disciplines in a step-by-step process. The final part of this chapter suggests how you might go about this.
>
> Further information on each of these options, and how to deliver them, will be given in Chapter 8.

6
REACHING OUT
- WHO IS GOING TO SUPPORT US?

Drawing up a prospect list of possible funders is one of the first steps in raising funds. Indeed, whatever your school's location or situation, there will be funders willing to support you. The key is to identify the funders who will most likely give. So if you feel your parents will not be able to give much because of lack of disposable income, the chances are that a number of trusts and foundations will want to hear from you (many such bodies supporting schools in deprived areas).

Ethical considerations
i. Acceptance policy
Before you begin selecting prospects, it is worth creating a written policy on the types of donors you are and are not willing to accept support. This helps in a number of ways including:

- Saving time researching potential prospects that prove to be incompatible with the school's ethical stance
- Avoiding having to turn down donors directly, where a policy would have meant they were either not approached or were told from the outset that a donation was not suitable
- Ensuring that all your school's fundraisers are aware of what is and is not allowed, irrespective of their own, differing ethical positions.

ii. Questions to ask
When discussing your ethical policy, you should cover three overarching topics.

- Types of organisation
- Types of activity
- Financial checks

Types of organisation
Consider whether you would accept donations from these kinds of organisation (as well as any other issues that would concern you):
- Alcohol and tobacco companies
- Arms companies

- A company that uses children to manufacture its goods
- A company that knowingly damages the environment
- Companies that manufacture sweets or junk food.

Types of activity

While most fundraising activities are fairly harmless, some do cause concerns for certain people. So determine whether you would be happy to accept funds from activities such as these:

- A company giving you money in return for access to the school's parents
- A company selling its products and giving you a percentage of any sales
- An individual with controversial views, such as a member of the British National Party, running the marathon in order to raise money for you.

Financial checks

Occasionally, you might be fortunate enough to receive support or a donation which is either unusual or unexpected in its size. While there is a good chance that this is legitimate, there is also a chance that something is not quite right. For instance, some unethical companies have been known to make incredible offers of support in the hope that they will pick up benefits (such as new customers) before reneging on the actual donation.

You might therefore wish to make it a policy to take a couple of references (one financial and one personal) from anybody who makes a donation above a certain size. You could make an exception to certain organisations, such as listed companies, so that it did not lead to needless checking. The advantage of doing this is that you can ask for such things quite innocently by saying that it is a procedure you have to follow. Conversely, if you have no such policy such a request could cause offence for an innocent party (or feigned offence for a not so innocent one).

iii. Final decision

There are no correct answers to the above questions, but they can lead to heated debate. One person's ethics can be very far removed from another's, yet people often assume that their position is the most reasonable. You will normally be able to work out your position through discussion and debate but, if not, then you should have an ultimate arbitrator, such as the head teacher or chair of governors. Once that person decides, everyone must fall into line!

Potential donors you might approach
To begin with, list anybody that you think might give to your school. There will be four major categories.

i. Individuals
Types
- Ex-pupils / alumni
- Governors
- Parents
- Local people
- Members of the public with a particular interest in your project
- Famous or well-to-do people with a link to your school (e.g. the local MP)

Suitable fundraising activities

Newsletter; Website; Events; Raffles and lotteries; Recycling; Community fundraisers; Major donor fundraising; Company fundraising (that is introductions to the relevant people at their places of work); Social media; Text giving; Legacies

Where to find?
- Your database
- Facebook
- LinkedIn
- Local newspaper
- Door-to-door campaign
- Sunday Times Rich List (Most charities use this as a source of prospects so you will need a 'hook' or link to your school in order to stand out)
- Via governors and other well-connected people within your school community
- Networking events, particularly prestigious local ones

6. Reaching out - who is going to support us?

ii. Businesses
Types
- Local businesses
- National businesses with an interest in the area you are supporting
- Businesses of ex-pupils
- Businesses where parents work
- Businesses owned by parents

Suitable fundraising activities
Newsletter; Website; Events; Raffles and lotteries; Recycling; Community fundraisers; Company fundraising; Cause related marketing

Where to find?
- Local Business Guides (e.g. www.yell.com)
- Companygiving.org.uk provides giving details of approximately 500 companies (www.companygiving.org.uk)
- The Guide to UK Company Giving also gives details of approximately 500 companies (www.dsc.org.uk)
- Academies with sponsors and Trust schools which have businesses on their governing bodies should certainly consider approaches to their corporate partners and supply chains
- Communications, such as through your newsletter or website, to parents
- The 'Corporate Social Responsibility' pages of large companies
- A Google search for local people and businesses
- A simple walk down your local high street
- Your local MP – simply ask your representative to let any suitable companies he or she comes across know that you are interested in partnering.

iii. Trusts and foundations
Types
- Local trusts
- National trusts
- Livery companies
- Rotary Clubs

Suitable fundraising activities
Newsletter; Trust applications; Sponsorship

Where to find?
There are approximately 200 big national trusts and foundations, along with thousands of smaller ones. These latter funders are often very small and only support local charities and organisations. So if you find one that supports your area then there is a good chance of success.

- Trustfunding.org.uk is a comprehensive directory of trusts and foundations from the Directory of Social Change (DSC)
- The DSC also produces an annual Guide to Educational Grants giving details of almost 1,400 educational trusts (www.dsc.org.uk)
- Your local rotary club might well give support: www.rotary.org/myrotary/en/take-action/apply-grants
- See Resources section (Chapter 17) for details of other list providers.

iv. Statutory
Types
- Local government
- National government

Suitable fundraising activities
Newsletter; Trust and statutory applications

Where to find?
In addition to the Education & Skills Funding Agency (www.gov.uk/government/organisations/education-and-skills-funding-agency) you could subscribe to www.governmentfunding.org.uk which provides details of a range of local, regional and national government grants.

Donor motivations
As well as knowing who might give to your school, you also need to work out why they will give to you. This might seem daunting as there are hundreds of reasons why people and organisations give. However, these can be distilled down into four main reasons: *philanthropic, affinity, social and mutual benefit*.

These motivations are pivotal to how you approach and interact with donors, and it is the understanding of this fact that particularly marks out the professional fundraiser from the amateur. The latter approaches every prospect the same way (normally by explaining why funding is needed and then asking for a contribution) while the former is constantly assessing prospects' motivations. The reason why the professional's approach is so much more successful is that quite often your biggest donors might have no interest in your school *per se* and will instead be attracted by other factors. To understand why this might be, it is worth explaining the four motivations to giving.

i. Philanthropic

This motivation revolves around doing good deeds and giving something back. It focuses on improving society and helping the needy. For most people, it is perhaps the truest form of giving as there is little or no vested interest behind it. Instead there is a sense of duty or moral imperative to give.

Most religions embody this motivation. For example, Tzedakah and Zakat are central pillars of Judaism and Islam respectively and stress a duty to support those in need. The charity donor supporting a portfolio of charities would similarly be giving under this motivation.

> **Example donors**
> - Trusts and foundations with general charitable purposes as their stated objects
> - Those of a religious persuasion (but see *affinity* motivation)
> - Those who have been very successful and attribute part of that success to outside help.

ii. Affinity

Those of this motivation believe fully in the project that you are putting to them. For instance, a scientist who gives to a science project is likely to do so because he or she believes in the project itself, rather than for any other reason. As its name implies, those falling under this motivation are likely to fully understand the rationale behind a project and be equally as supportive as you are.

A lot of schools assume that every donor falls under this motivation. That leads to two kinds of problem. Either the arguments put forward for giving leave a good many people unmoved or fundraising is only focused on those who display this motivation (normally parents). Both scenarios lead to a lot of lost giving as those who might give, but who fall under different motivational categories, never feel compelled to support.

In terms of numbers of donors, the majority will come under *affinity*. (That does not necessarily mean that you will raise the most support from this motivational group – one large donor with, say, a *mutual benefit* motivation, could be more than able to match hundreds of gifts of fully supportive parents.)

Example donors
- Ex-pupils who have done very well and have a fondness for their school
- Ex-pupils who have done very well but may have left school early – they often seem to regret this and wish to show their old establishment that they have made something of themselves!
- Local businesses
- Local people
- Local trusts
- (Some) parents.

iii. Mutual benefit

Those falling under this motivation want something in return for giving. While it could be argued that every donor wants something in return (for example, someone giving as part of a religious duty is still asking to be considered a good follower of that religion) when we talk of *mutual benefit* here we are usually referring to business benefits. Giving to the local school confers a number of these, such as valuable publicity, access to new customers and raised brand awareness.

Not everyone is comfortable with this motivation. For example, the Friends of one London school successfully negotiated a sponsorship deal with a local estate agent for the summer fete. With several thousands of pounds invested, the business sent a representative, who in turn had the misfortune to be castigated by one angry parent for 'taking advantage of my child to make profit!' Still, if you are happy to offer benefits in return for support (see page 27 for more on ethical considerations) then you are potentially tapping into much larger purses.

Example donors
- Local businesses
- National businesses

iv. Social

Those motivated by the *social* factor want their giving to make them look good and have others recognise them for that giving. Any donation is considered on the impact it will have on the donor's status.

This motivation is surprisingly common - after all, who does not like being recognised? However few people will admit to it. In practice, I would assume that someone is likely to be motivated by it unless proven otherwise!

Example donors
- Ex-pupils
- Local business leaders
- (Some) parents.

These motivations are extremely important and will help inform later fundraising stages, such as writing proposals and thanking donors. Awareness of these concepts avoids the one-size-fits-all approach which will seriously curb your income potential. Remember as well that a lot of donors will have more than one motivation, with *affinity* and *social* being very common amongst the school community.

Chapter 6 in a nutshell

The chapter considers how to identify the key sources of financial support for the school starting, importantly, with examination of unacceptable sources.

Four main categories of funder – individuals, businesses, trusts and foundations and statutory grant making bodies – are considered and the various means of accessing them described.

Finally, the chapter emphasises the importance of maximising donors' engagement by understanding what motivates their giving.

7
MAKING THE APPROACH

Blanket approach versus personalised approach

Once you have a list of likely funders, you will need to narrow it down to a manageable level. Do this by breaking the prospect list down into two groups. The first will be those large enough to warrant individual attention; these are your major donors. The second will be those who are likely to support you but whose individual donations will be relatively small, so that any extra effort you put into this group is unlikely to result in much more income. These are your generic groups.

i. Major donors

By defining what size of donor you would consider giving personalised or individualised attention to, you effectively determine who your major donors will be. Some of these will never have given anything to you but will have the potential to give you a sizeable sum. The common factor amongst this group is that to unlock the higher giving levels, you will need to provide a tailored and customised approach.

As a rough rule of thumb, anybody giving you a four-figure sum should receive a degree of personalised attention. The amount of attention that you give depends on how many such donors of that level you have – a few and you can probably go and visit each individually to see if they will give more; a lot and a signed thank-you letter from the head teacher might be best. Of course, regardless of how much attention you are able to give your donors, it is important that you keep in regular contact with them over time in order to develop a strong long-term relationship.

It is also likely that there will be one or two prospects who will never give you very much money but who, because of their influence or importance, should be treated as major donors. For instance, you might meet a school governor individually because their address book could open up many more contacts for you, even though they themselves might only be inclined to give very little.

ii. Generic groups

The giving capacity of the majority of your prospects will be too small to justify personalised attention. However, it is usually easy enough to lump such small donors into groups that share enough common characteristics to make generic approaches. For instance, most parents will give relatively small sums of money and you will certainly not have the time or inclination to go and see each one.

However, you can safely assume that nearly all of these parents will be motivated by the *affinity* motivation (see page 32 above). So communications and activities that appeal as such should cover all members of this group. In other words, lump them together as one group: Parents.

Similarly, you might not have time to speak to lots of local businesses, whereas a letter drop might be feasible. Given that most such businesses will be looking to increase the number of local people using their services, a generic appeal concentrating on this aspect should suffice.

Alumni, past donors and local residents are other prospect types which might be best served as generic categories.

Type of approach

Once you have narrowed down your prospect list into manageable segments, you can think about how you will make initial contact with each.

The guiding principle on approaches is that the more face-to-face, individualised contact you have with a donor the more likely you are to gain a donation and a bigger one at that. However, this needs to be balanced with the feasibility of meeting lots of people face-to-face and any constrictions put on you by the donor themselves, such as trusts that will only accept written applications. All things considered, if there is a choice and you can accommodate it then go for more face-to-face interaction.

Bearing in mind the above rule, virtually all of your prospects will be contacted or approached in one of the ways described below. These are listed with the most interactive, that is to say effective, at the top.

i. Meetings
   Good for
- Major donors
- Detailed or complex partnerships
- Companies
- Trust and foundations (though it can be difficult to obtain meetings with these bodies)

   Bad for
- Small donors
- Simple donations

ii. Phone calls
Good for
- Major donors you cannot meet, particularly lower-level ones
- Companies
- Trusts and foundations (i.e. checking that it is worth applying)
- Livery companies
- Alumni
- Governors

Bad for
- Parents (unless major donors)
- Small donors

iii. Events
Good for
- Small donors, such as parents and local residents
- Alumni
- Local businesses
- Local foundations

Bad for
- Trusts and foundations

iv. Raffles
Good for
- Small donors, such as parents and local residents
- Companies (for prizes)
- Alumni
- Governors

Bad for
- Trusts and foundations
- Livery companies

v. Applications
Good for
- Trusts and foundations
- Companies
  (It is even better to meet or call such organisations before applying!)

Bad for
- Individuals, such as parents (assuming that you can apply to such people!)

vi. Social media
Good for
- Alumni
- Parents
- Local residents

Bad for
- Major donors
- Trusts and foundations
- Companies
- Livery companies

vii. Written communications
Good for
- Alumni
- Parents
- Local residents

Bad for

You might have no choice, but try not to write 'cold' to any of the following:
- Large companies
- Trusts and foundations
- Livery companies
- Major donors

Determining who will make the approach

Now that you have a more manageable list of prospects and an idea of how you are going to engage them, you can work out who should be the lead person for each prospect or prospect group. For example, while the majority of parental approaches can be left to other parents, unlocking sizeable gifts from major donors will probably need the involvement of senior leaders within the school.

Factors to take into account when assigning people to lead include Time factors, Donor motivations, Peer-to-peer giving and Impact.

i. Time factors
It is certainly worth considering how much time a given individual can offer. For instance, while the head teacher might be the most desirable person to make an approach, this may be unrealistic given their schedule.

ii. Donor motivations
Donor motivations, as discussed on page 31, are also helpful in determining who should be involved in bringing on a prospect.

Those of the *affinity* persuasion are likely to be influenced by seeing pupils themselves, while parents are likely to readily empathise with other parents. Where a prospect is motivated by the *social* factor, then a meeting involving the chair of governors, head teacher or any important person linked to your school would be advisable. Discussions with those with an interest in the *mutual benefit* side will be better served by meeting the bursar, school business manager or anyone with a commercial background. If you plan to meet someone motivated in a *philanthropic* sense then involving a religious figure, such as a chaplain, imam or rabbi, might be appropriate.

iii. Peer-to-peer giving
The rationale behind this factor is that individuals generally respond most enthusiastically to one of their peers. For instance, the fact that parents respond well to other parents is one reason behind the PTA movement.

So for each of your prospect groups consider if there is somebody who would fit into that group within your school community and make the request on your behalf. For instance, a local business supporter would be a good person to make requests to other local businesses, while an ex-pupil would likely have impact with other alumni.

If there is no direct link then consider equivalences. For instance, the head teacher leads the school and so should probably meet the chief executive of a trust or company, who in turn leads his or her organisation. Similarly, school business managers should probably meet with corporate finance directors.

iv. Impact
Be mindful of the impact and value that the person making the funding request can have. For instance, large donations can be complex, both in negotiation and form. In such cases, it can take several meetings to pin down details and determine the overall size of gift. If your head teacher is involved from the outset then you miss out on his or her impact later on,

when an appearance might be needed to push negotiations over the finish line.

Similarly, try to build in a degree of flexibility with your most impactful people. For instance, an unexpected major donor might request an impromptu meeting with senior staff. You will therefore want to make sure that the senior team is already warm to your fundraising efforts and can accommodate such a wish.

Timing your approaches
The final element in planning your approaches is to timetable them. Two elements play into your timings: your schedule (internal factors) and those of your prospects (external factors).

i. Internal
Having an idea of how many engagement activities, such as major donor meetings or PTA events, that you can carry out each month, will give you an indication of when you can undertake your fundraising. For instance, the first week of term is likely to be off-limits for most school staff.

ii. External
Companies, along with trusts and foundations, will usually tell you when you need to apply. On the other hand, individuals are more varied and it is often a question of asking or making educated guesses. For instance, Christmas is usually a good time to engage parents as many will visit the school; this is particularly true of primaries.

Working out the time of approaches from the outset also helps you to theme approaches. For instance, social media, particularly for new parents, is likely to be more effective as the year progresses and people become more familiar with the school and get to know each other.

Bringing everything together
Having worked out all the above details, you will be able to produce three tables that will make clear to everyone involved in fundraising what is needed through the year. These three documents are:

- A timetable of activities
- A major donor prospect list
- A fundraiser's list of prospects.

i. Timetable of activities

This timetable gives an overview of all fundraising activities through the year. Not only does this help you visually check that you have a balance but also enables those involved in fundraising to see quickly when times will be busy.

	Activity	Donor Class	Lead	Expected amount
Sept	Welcome letter	Parents, local residents	Head	-
Oct	Halloween event	Parents, local residents	PTA	£5,000
	Major donor meetings	Major donors	Chair of Governors/ Head	£4,000
	Trust applications	Trusts and foundations, livery companies	Deputy Head	£10,000
Nov	Raffle	Parents, local residents	PTA	£4,000
Dec	Xmas Mailer	Parents, local residents	PTA	£2,000
Jan	Major donor meetings	Major donors	Chair of Governors/ Head	£5,000
Feb	Trust applications	Trusts and foundations, livery companies	Deputy Head	£20,000
Mar	Major donor meetings	Major donors	Chair of Governors/ Head	£10,000
Apr	Raffle	Parents, local residents	PTA	£7,000
May	Pupil fundraising	Parents, local residents	Year Head	£6,000
June	Major donor meetings	Major donors	Chair of Governors/ Head	£6,000
July	End-of-year letter	Parents, local residents	Head	£2,500

Table 2 Timetable of activities

ii. A major donor prospect list

	Interest	Capability	Likelihood	Motivation	Cash potential	Type of approach	Person making approach	Time of approach
George Young	7	3	8	Affinity	£4,000	Face-to-face	Head teacher	Nov
Mr and Mrs Lakhtl	5	2	10	Social and Affinity	£2,000	Telephone call	Bursar	Nov
Angela Ryan	8	3	5	Philanthropic	£4,500	Letter	Bursar	Dec
Greenfingers Gardening	6	9	1	Mutual Benefit	£5,000	Face-to-face	Chair of Governors	Oct
Parents	n/a	n/a	n/a	Affinity	£25,000		PTA	Sept onwards
Alumni	n/a	n/a	n/a	Affinity	£10,000		Deputy Head	Sept onwards

Table 3 Major donor prospect list

iii. A fundraiser's list of prospects

	Interest	Capability	Likelihood	Motivation	Approach	Date of Approach
George Young	7	3	8	Affinity	Meeting	Jan
Mr and Mrs Lakhtl	5	2	10	Social and Affinity	Phone call	Mar

Table 4 Head teacher prospect list

7. Making the approach

Chapter 7 in a nutshell

Having considered in Chapter 6 who should be approached for funding, this chapter describes the mechanics of making approaches. How should they be made, by whom, and when?

A set of tables are proposed for organising this part of the fundraising drive.

8
THE FUNDRAISING DISCIPLINES

Finally, in this chapter, we come to fundraising as most people will understand it, and look in detail at each of the topics outlined in Chapter 5. You could start at this point and indeed many schools will do so but the more effort you have put into the previous stages the more successful you will eventually be. We will discuss each technique in turn, starting with what we suggest are the easiest and most essential.

Newsletter
i. Purpose
The best newsletters have a clear purpose. From a fundraising point of view, they should:

- Recognise and reward
- Move fundraising goals forward

Recognition and reward
Naturally, your donors should be recognised in your newsletters unless they have made it clear that they do not want any publicity. As a result, you should try and name-check all your new major donors – a simple list of people and organisations can be enough when you have a large number.

For your biggest benefactors, you should consider writing a case-study. Not only does this make the supporter feel important but it also raises the aspirations of donors currently giving a level or two below. However the size of the grant should not always be your determining factor as to who is recognised in your newsletters. For instance, you might wish to encourage a particular group to become more involved, such as hard-to-reach parents. That might mean including a special thank you in the language of a particular ethnic group that has contributed more than normal. By showcasing examples of these smaller types of donor, as well as different ways of supporting, you encourage others to do similarly.

Of course, a major donor could easily surpass the contribution of a thousand parents so never skimp on their recognition.

Advancing fundraising goals
Your newsletter serves as a valuable instrument to further your fundraising efforts. Publicising new campaigns, ensuring milestones are met and energising donors are some of the goals you might wish to set.

Even if not explicitly spelt out, try and allow readers to be able to answer these questions by reading your newsletter:

- What is the problem being overcome?
- What is the solution?
- Why should I support?
- How can I get involved?

In addition, do not forget to put timescales in place. If you are looking to raise a 7-figure sum for a new building, how long is it going to take? If you are not explicit, readers will answer such questions for themselves and not necessarily correctly. For instance, if their answer is 'That money will never be raised' then you will gain no funding!

ii. Features
Stylistic points
- Use no more than two colours
- Stick to one or two fonts and no more than three sizes
- Use italics and boldface to emphasise points
- Do not be afraid to have plenty of empty space
- Ensure photos and pictures are neither too large to overwhelm nor too small to be effective
- Keep newsletters concise – four to six pages maximum
- Ensure that e-newsletters can be read conveniently on mobiles and tablets (consider a hosted e-newsletter service if you do not have the technical skills to do this yourself)
- Use buttons and icons, rather than text, for links wherever possible

Content points
- Translate smaller donations into tangible benefits, particularly if you have a large overall target. For example, '£50 = 2 hours of Code Club; £10 = 1 Coding Book for a Child'
- Use lots of pictures of volunteers, donors and of course children (but see Using photographs, page 48 below)
- People like to be recognised – name donors and volunteers generously

- Give examples of recent donations, including all your major ones
- Highlight different types of support that you would welcome, such as volunteering time, thus connecting with parents and others who are not willing or do not have the capacity to give financially
- Encourage readers to go back to your website
- Enable readers to give easily, such as a 'donate now' button on digital communications or website details for hard copy newsletters
- Provide a personalised message from the person in charge of fundraising
- Consider including screenshots that link to video content on your website where readers might give
- Provide a mechanism for people to contact you with questions, comments or suggestions

Distribution
- Address the newsletter to a named individual if possible rather than 'Dear Parent' or 'Dear Supporter'
- Aim to send regularly, at least once a term
- Experiment with the time and frequency that you send your newsletter. This will help maximise engagement levels
- Keep subject lines short to optimise opening rates on digital devices, such as smart phones and tablets
- Add e-newsletter opt-ins to every page of your website
- Ask followers and friends on other social media, such as Facebook and Twitter, to sign up to your newsletter. Time-sensitive posts can be particularly effective, for instance: 'New newsletter tomorrow – sign up here!'
- If you are still sending PDFs via email then seriously consider signing up to one of the hosted e-newsletter services.

iii. Hosted e-newsletter services
Hosted e-newsletter services are extremely helpful in setting out your content and managing your distribution lists. They are quick and easy for the lay person to understand and operate, yet provide a level of sophistication that would have cost thousands of pounds just a few years ago.

Aweber (www.aweber.com), GetResponse (www.getresponse.com) or MailChimp (www.mailchimp.com) are three potential providers. The last of these has a free option for those with up to 2,000 subscribers and 12,000 emails a month.

From a fundraising point of view, perhaps the most useful feature of these services is the ability to track those who are, and are not, engaged. Those who are opening and passing on your newsletter a lot can potentially be asked more often for a donation. For those who never open your newsletters, you might wish to try a different approach. For example, if language levels are an issue then you might ask a parent to produce a translated copy.

iv. Using photographs

There are a variety of rules and regulations which should be followed in terms of using photographs in newsletters. These come under two categories: safeguarding and data protection.

Safeguarding of children and young people

The NSPCC provides a helpful factsheet covering this area: www.nspcc.org.uk/preventing-abuse/safeguarding/photography-sharing-images-guidance/ In particular:

- Do not publish any personal details of any child or young person
- Do not use real-life pictures of any of your children or young people to highlight a service that might be deemed negative, such as a reading partner scheme for weak readers. Use stock pictures instead.
- Do not use pictures of your children undertaking activities such as swimming which could be misused in the wrong hands.

Data protection

If not already doing so, the school should be gaining consent from parents and guardians for the usage of photographs in publications at the start of the school year. This should be enough, unless the pictures were taken at an event run by a third party when consent needs to be given again. The school should have someone with overall responsibility for data protection so check with that person that your newsletters comply with the rules.

In terms of adults, such as major donors, you should gain consent where those individuals are being named.

For more information on this area, have a look at the advice given by the Information Commissioner's Office (ICO):
ico.org.uk/for-the-public/schools/photos/
ico.org.uk/for-organisations/education/

In addition, if you have specific questions then call the ICO directly (Telephone number: 0303 123 1113).

Website

If you are serious about fundraising then you should dedicate a prominent section of your school's main website to the raising of support. Even if you are sending out newsletters or meeting with major donors and companies, prospective donors are likely to visit your website before committing.

i. Essentials
- Being able to take online payments is a *sine qua non*.
- Make sure the payment facility on your website accommodates Gift Aid – you are losing considerable amounts of money if not. (See page 92 for more details).
- Ensure people can sign up easily to your newsletter via your website (ideally on every page). Keeping the sign-up process simple will mean that you do not lose people as they work their way through (email address and name will probably suffice).
- If your website is very old then consider replacing it. For instance, building your own website is fairly simple these days (try www.wix.com, www.wordpress.com or www.moonfruit.com.) These can often be co-ordinated with e-newsletter providers, like MailChimp, saving you time and vastly improving the visitor experience.
- To benefit from all the features of a dedicated fundraising platform, provide links between your school website and the provider (try www.justgiving.com or www.schoolsfundingnetwork.co.uk).
- Ensure that the URL of your website is consistent with all your social media sites, so that if someone moves from, say, Twitter to your website they can be sure that it is the same school.

ii. Content
- Less is often more – do not cover your pages in text, nor with endless links or widgets.
- Try to keep content on one page to avoid the need for scrolling.
- Ensure that your home page is impactful, with large and striking images and minimal text.
- The top right-hand corner is the most important area of your website. Use it to plug your e-newsletter, 'donate now' button and other social media.

- Have a 'donate' button on every page, with a slightly more prominent one on the Homepage. Ensure that the link goes to a page able to process donations, not simply an information page.
- Consider replacing text-links with buttons wherever possible so as to reduce textual clutter.
- Ensure consistency in style across your site: content should be of the same font size, colour and layout throughout.
- Better to go for a tried-and-tested font, such as Arial, Times New Roman or Verdana.
- Avoid garish or unusual colours that will soon grate - black text on a white background is an effective option with wide appeal.
- Use bold for headlines.
- Keep bulleted items short.
- Give examples of what different levels of donations achieve. For example, '£100 enables us to run our breakfast club for one day', '£1,000 enables us to open 30 minutes earlier'.
- Have a unique identifier like your school logo across your web pages.
- Consider Search Engine Optimisation if you do not appear on the first page of a relevant Google search.
- Add social media icons linking to your other social media accounts, all of which should be driving fundraising.
- Video can add an extra dimension to a website but it needs to be of good quality.
- Ensure that your homepage stands out.

iii. Measurements

Knowing the effectiveness of your online presence is essential. To do this, you should be measuring two types of activity: website activity and giving amounts.

Website activity

Google Analytics allows you to measure activity on your website across a range of factors. For instance, you will be able to see which pages are most viewed, what links are clicked and when the site is most used. By looking at the details, you should be able to see what is, and is not, working well.

By focusing on one or two metrics, such as numbers of unique visitors or visits to individual pages, you can begin to make efforts to improve performance. Don't be worried if the absolute numbers are low at the start. The important point is to create an upward trend, which can take time. Eventually, you will reach the tipping point where word-of-mouth leads to a jump in usage.

To sign up to Google Analytics, which is free, go to: analytics.google.com

Giving amounts
How much money is being raised online every month? Is it going up year-on-year? These are key questions that you need to ask. For instance, if you raised £5,000 last December then you might aim for £6,000 this year. To achieve this, you might decide to give a bigger plug in your newsletter, an end-of-year pep talk from the head teacher and a special letter from the chair of governors.

In addition, are there any months where activity is particularly low? August will probably be a slow month but what about February? Is there anything that can be done then to raise the amounts given?

Community fundraising
Most schools, especially primaries, will be familiar with this area of fundraising. Nevertheless, it is important to ensure that activities are properly planned and that volunteers are kept motivated.

i. Types of activity
There are numerous community fundraising activities that can be undertaken, some on school premises and others outside.

Internal
Auctions, book sales, cake sales, easter egg hunts, fancy dress days, readathons, treasure hunts and of course simple bucket collections, to name but a few.

External
Marathons, triathlons, sponsored cycles, sponsored diets, swims and general fundraising.

ii. Inspiring your volunteers
It is important that there is good communication between those managing the school's overall fundraising and the volunteers undertaking the community fundraising. Here are some techniques to make that happen:

- Ensure that all volunteers are properly briefed. That includes informing helpers of the types of activity which have worked well in the past as well as passing on any technical or legal information, such as those involving Raffles (see page 60), Payroll Giving (see page 63) or Gift Aid (see page 92).
- Give out any materials that will help your community fundraisers, such as posters, badges, sponsorship forms or collecting buckets.
- Ensure that the school and the community fundraisers are in harmony and properly joined up. For instance, if everything is outsourced to the PTA at the start of year or class reps are nominated amongst the parents then try and arrange a private meeting with the head teacher at various times through the year, especially at the start and end. In addition, make sure that there is a quick and easy route for at least one community fundraiser to raise points and issues with the school.

iii. Sponsored activities

If your community fundraisers are willing to undertake marathons and other sponsored activities then make sure that they are maximising the income they raise. For example, if they plan to use JustGiving then make sure you have a school page set up, on which the community fundraisers can piggyback. They will then be able to Gift Aid money directly to your school.

If you are not set up in this way, then approach Schools Funding Network which can set up individual school campaigns under their charity on JustGiving and other sites. This takes care of the Gift Aid for you.

iv. Secondary activities

While your volunteers are raising funds, they could also be doing other activities. For instance, they could raise awareness of a capital campaign or alert people to classes and activities going on in the school. So make sure your community fundraisers are aware of these secondary activities.

v. More ideas

Inevitably, people run out of new ideas for community activities. One way to gain renewed vigour and fresh impetus is to look at the websites of major charities. There are normally a good number of interesting options to be found here. PTA UK (www.pta.org.uk) also offers ideas for fundraising.

Event fundraising

The majority of schools will run one or more events to raise funds and support. They are enjoyable and fun occasions with the potential to raise sizeable funds.

All events should comprise four stages, which we will run through below.

i. Pre-event
Objectives

The best events have pre-agreed objectives. These might well include cash targets but a wise fundraiser would include other elements as well. These might include:

- Awareness raising – letting parents and others know of your big fundraising needs, including new campaigns, would be one example of this.
- Bringing on new donors – it is easier to meet and talk with big donors by inviting them to something fun and neutral, such as your school fair, than it is to ask for a sponsorship meeting.
- Thanking existing supporters – acknowledging the support that has been given during the year demonstrates how much that funding is appreciated, thereby greatly increasing the odds of future support.
- Re-energising volunteers – voluntary helpers are often seen as a free resource. However, they usually need high levels of support and recognition if they are not to become disenchanted. A simple thank you from the head teacher at an event can be surprisingly powerful despite requiring minimal time and cost.

Naturally, objectives should be SMART ones:
- Specific – there is no ambiguity on what is required
- Measurable – there is a simple way of measuring whether the objective has been met or not
- Assignable – someone has overall responsibility for the objective
- Realistic – the objective can be achieved given the available resources
- Time-related – there is a deadline for when the objective should be met.

Tasks

Once you have your objectives (ideally two or three items), you should define the tasks needed to fulfil them. These should be updated as you go along, ideally at regular planning meetings. For instance:

Objective 1: Thank major donors
- Head teacher to thank G.Young and MM Building Society
- Chair of governors to thank P. Ling and Fairwell Estates

A good many schools will have parents with project management skills or experience of running events. So put out a request if you are running any sizeable event and then use the help of any suitable volunteers.

ii. During the event

While you will no doubt have specific activities in mind, from musical soirées to sports days, from a fundraising point of view you will want to have someone overseeing donor relations and keeping a record of follow-up actions.

Event co-ordinator

While everyone involved in the event should know their individual tasks, one person should be responsible for the day's overall success. Having such a person removes unnecessary stresses and ensures that objectives are met. Types of task this person might perform include:

- Ensuring all VIPs are looked after – while individual dignitaries might have a certain member of staff allocated to them, having someone in overall control provides a second line of support if required.
- Ensuring all guests are enjoying themselves – staff and volunteers can be redeployed as required.
- Helping out where needed – there are always times when an extra pair of hands is called for!

iii. Capturing information

Good events invariably result in a lot of opportunities. In order that these are taken up post-event, ensure that the following two activities are being performed (ideally with one person co-ordinating):

Gathering names of those attending

Anybody attending the event is showing a degree of interest in the school. It is therefore likely that this group will respond more positively to your fundraising messages and that there might well be one or more potential large donors within the group. A simple way to gather names, if it is not clear who is who, is to have a prize draw for everybody who gives their details.

Noting down actions
A successful fundraising event provides a wealth of new information. For instance, a major prospect might express a passion for music and this will inform future funding requests to this person. So ensure that everyone has a means of taking down such details as it is easy to forget them during the course of an event.

One technique some fundraisers use when dealing with a lot of people is to write down a defining characteristic of each person they have met. For instance, 'Brian Kendall, garish tie, breeds rabbits, interested in the music studio' will trigger a memory of that person much more clearly than his unmarked business card.

iv. Post-event
Follow-up actions
Ideally, a new set of objectives and tasks should be set post-event. This might include items such as ensuring that all prospect leads are followed up in the next month, or completing Gift Aid paperwork.

Measurements
The measurements agreed pre-event should be collected. As well as overall amounts raised, most professional fundraisers would look at the following items:

- Costs, including staff time
- Net profitability (many seemingly successful events fall down considerably when this is taken into account)
- Number of guests
- Number of major donors attending
- Number of follow-up funding meetings and opportunities.

Once you have the information, analyse it for improvements. For instance, if you invited a number of local businesses but none turned up, was this because the invitations went out too late or because the fundraising elements of the event were over-emphasised at the expense of relationship-building?

Above all, try to keep your measurement criteria similar from year to year. This allows trends to be spotted in good time. After all, if an event raises £10,000 it is difficult to say whether that is good, bad or indifferent – you need to see previous years' data.

Trust and statutory applications

If you can master this area of fundraising then you will have mastered the area which traditionally gives the biggest return on investment. We run through the key points to successful applications below.

i. Eligibility

Before you even begin to apply, make sure that you fit the criteria. This might seem an obvious statement to make but funders continually complain that they are inundated with applications that they could never support because they are outside their guidelines. So do not waste time on a speculative approach just because the sums being offered are large – if you have any doubt, ask the funder directly before you begin writing!

ii. Structure

Where there are guidelines or a set application which you need to fill in, provide the information requested. Give real thought as to what is being asked of you and what the funder is looking for in beneficiaries. One way of doing this is by using the same language and jargon as the funder.

Where there are no guidelines then follow the structure below. It will provide you with a foolproof format for presenting your funding needs. It avoids common mistakes, such as producing proposals that are too long or missing important pieces of information.

The standard proposal should have the following headings:

1. Summary
2. Background
3. The project
4. Budget
5. Benefits
6. Conclusion
7. Contact details

Your proposal should cover no more than two pages. Even if you are seeking a 6 or 7-figure donation, the initial proposal should be short, simply seeking to pique the funder's interest before more detailed discussions can take place. Being concise is a key fundraising skill!

The individual sections of the proposal will now be discussed below.

1. Summary

This should be one to two paragraphs long. Explain what you are aiming to do and why. Be clear what you are looking for and outline any benefits you are offering in return. Try and include a little information about the school so it is identifiable but keep this brief.

From your summary, the reader should be able to determine whether the proposition is the kind of thing they will or will not fund. You therefore need to include most of your best points because if the funder is not taken immediately then there is a good chance they will not read the rest. Here is an example of how to do it:

'Greenfields is an outstanding primary school based in Lambeth in London. We are raising funds for a school playground to provide a richer learning environment and to encourage our children to be more active. We are seeking £15,675 to finance the work. As a funder of healthy living in the borough, we believe this project will be an excellent fit for your charitable objects.'

2. Background

Explain what issue or problem you are trying to solve. One or two paragraphs are all that is needed and bullet points are often helpful. If you can call on external evidence to explain why this is indeed an issue, then all the better. Remember to remove all jargon unless the funder uses such terminology themselves. For example:

Our current playground is completely tarmacked, with no trees or plants. This causes the following issues:

- *Children cutting and grazing themselves*
- *Limited play activities*
- *A sterile environment devoid of wildlife*
- *A negative environment that does not enhance education (a recent report by the Department for Education highlighted the benefits of a rich playground environment).*

3. The project

In a paragraph or two explain what your project involves and how it addresses the problem. Again, bullets can be helpful. Provide details of any notable developments or successes in relation to the project so far, such as money already raised. Give an idea of timescale and explain how you are going to ensure that the project will be successful when completed. This might include regular monitoring for instance.

For example:

Our proposed new playground has been designed by an ex-pupil who is now working in landscaping. It has been designed with the following bespoke features:

- *Separate areas for ball games, quiet reflection and eating*
- *Wildlife-friendly plants and shrubs*
- *Eco-friendly play equipment, including tree cabin*
- *We have negotiated a 20% discount from the equipment providers to reduce our funding needs and hope to complete the 4-week turn-around by the New Year.*

4. Budget

State how much funding you need, with three to four budget lines. Make sure this doesn't end in a round number, like £10,000, otherwise funders will doubt that this is a real or thought-out figure. In other words, they will be inclined to give less and might not give at all. For example:

Tarmac removal	*£6,900*
Plants and shrubs	*£2,300*
Playground equipment	*£23,475*
Total	**£32,675**

We have raised £17,000 already and hope that you can provide the remaining £15,675.

5. Benefits

You should explain the benefits to the donor of supporting this project. This will likely be different from the benefits you are going to derive, which will be outlined in 'The project' section. Remember the four donor motivations (*affinity, philanthropic, social* and *mutual benefit*). For instance, if your donor is looking for prestige or something in return then you will need to cover it in this section.

Here is an example of how you might write this section:

The benefits of supporting our new playground include:

- *Supporting your stated claim of enhancing wildlife*
- *Having naming rights to the playground*
- *Generating considerable goodwill amongst the school community*
- *Writing a piece in our school newsletter going to all parents.*

6. Conclusion

The conclusion should be one to two short paragraphs. It needs to explain why action is needed now, rather than at some vague time in the future. It also needs to emphasise why this is a unique project worthy of support. After all, for all you know, the funder might have lots of proposals to consider!

If this a prelude to a large funding request then specifically ask for a meeting at this point, along the lines of 'We hope this paper gives you a sense of our ambitions and look forward to discussing the plans in more detail at a suitable time'.

Here is an example of how you might end a proposal:

'If we can raise the required money in the next six weeks then we will be able to complete the work over the holidays, ensuring minimum disruption to our children. It will also allow the many people coming to our spring fête to see the work you have enabled first-hand and express their thanks. We therefore hope that you will be able to bring this about and make a lot of adults and children very happy indeed.'

7. Contact details

Finally ensure that you have your contact details written down – you never know who the proposal is going to be passed on to and who might want to contact you. Ensure that this is a real person, ideally someone with a degree of responsibility – people rarely offer large sums of money if the contact address starts admin@.... or reception@....!

iii. Following up
It is surprising how often funders can forget proposals, often because they have so many to look at. So once you have sent in your application or proposal, leave a certain amount of time and then follow up. When making such calls, try and find out the following:

- Whether the proposal will be taken forward
- Whether any further information is needed
- When a decision is likely

All being well, you will receive your funding at which point you will likely have to agree to certain terms and conditions. Comply with these and give regular updates, even if these are not formally requested. If the funder sees you as a reliable and helpful beneficiary, it will increase your chances of success considerably the next time you apply.

If you are turned down, try and find out why. If you can overcome the issues raised then you might be successful the next time.

Raffles and lotteries
These are excellent ways to raise funds and the chances are that you will already be running one in some shape or form.

i. Tickets
You can make your own tickets but it's often simpler to buy some. Try your high street or an online provider, such as www.raffleticketsdirect.co.uk or www.whsmith.co.uk/products/whsmith-raffle-tickets-pack-of-1000/395823

ii. Prizes
Prizes are relatively easy to source. Most companies, for instance, are much happier giving prizes than money, particularly if you have not yet built up a relationship with them.

iii. Licences and other regulations
It is beyond the scope of this book to explain all the regulations behind running lotteries and raffles. What we will do however is explain the overarching requirements and direct you to the correct place, if necessary, to apply for licences or find other information.

Raffles and lotteries fall into two main categories: those where you sell tickets before and during the event and those where you only sell tickets during it. The former requires a licence, while the latter does not.

Lottery with no ticket sales pre-event
- All tickets must be sold at the location and the draw must take place during the event, which may last more than a single day.
- The promoters of the lottery may not deduct more than £100 from the proceeds in respect of the expenses incurred in organising the lottery, such as the cost of printing tickets, hire of equipment and so on.
- No more than £500 can be spent on prizes (but other prizes may be donated to the lottery)
- The lottery cannot involve a rollover of prizes from one lottery to another.

Lottery, with pre-event ticket sales, where the total value of tickets put on sale does not exceed £20,000 (or £250,000 in any one calendar year)
- You will need to contact your local licensing authority and pay for a licence (if you are not sure how to do this go to www.gov.uk/find your-local-council and enter your local authority. Once you have found that then simply search for 'Lotteries and Raffles').
- Your local authority will provide detailed guidance on the rules governing this type of lottery. Bear in mind as well that lottery tickets must not be sold to, or by, those under the age of 16.
- If you find that ticket sales are going exceptionally well and you are likely to surpass the £20,000 limit then you will need to apply to the Gambling Commission (i.e. the lottery-type described below).

Lottery, with pre-event ticket sales, where total ticket proceeds exceed £20,000
- Regulations are fairly onerous and you will need to apply to the Gambling Commission.
- www.gamblingcommission.gov.uk/for-gambling-businesses/for-gambling-businesses.aspx provides all the information for this type of lottery, including application details.
- If your lottery is likely to reach this size, you might find it easier to employ an outside agency to help (e.g. www.woodsgroup.co.uk/)

iv. Marketing
If you are running a lottery where you are selling tickets before the event then you will need to target potential buyers. To do this well, you should answer the following questions:

Who will sell tickets?
The more people you have selling tickets the better. This might include staff at the front gate, parents selling to other parents and local residents, or school suppliers asking their staff whether they would like to take part.

Setting a target for each seller is one way to ensure high numbers. Having a competition with a reward for the highest ticket seller is another way to incentivise sales.

Who will we target?
Local residents, parents, local businesses, staff of companies where your parents work and your school suppliers are all possible buyers of your ticket. The most important point is to simply take every opportunity to sell tickets, though remember that you cannot sell tickets to those under 16 years of age. Every adult you come across is effectively fair game!

Recycling as a fundraiser
While recycling items will never make huge sums for your school, when combined with the environmental and educational aspects, it certainly becomes a worthwhile activity. We run through the various items you can recycle, along with the main service providers, below.

i. What can be recycled for money?
Most recyclable items can be sold to raise funds. Specialist organisations cater for the following items, with the amount you might receive in brackets:

- Recycle inkjet cartridges (c. 80p each) www.recyclingforschools.co.uk or www.takeback.ltd.uk/schools/schools.aspx
- Aluminium cans (c. 45p for 70) www.thinkcans.net/ or call your local scrap metal merchant
- Mobile phones and other gadgets (average £25) www.money4urmobile.com or uk.webuy.com
- CDs and DVDs (You will need the barcode. Average £1) www.musicmagpie.co.uk or uk.webuy.com

- Books: (Approximately 20% of RRP on newish books) www.webuybooks.co.uk or www.ziffit.com/sell-my-books
- Paper (you will need a lot to make this worthwhile!) www.collectandrecycle.com/services/cardboard-and-paper-recycling

ii. Recycling for charities

Of course, you might prefer to simply recycle your items through a mainstream charity. Most will be only too happy to take your items to fund their work. For instance, try

- Age UK: www.ageuk.org.uk/get-involved/make-a-donation/donate-to-our-shops/what-you-can-donate-to-an-age-uk-shop/ (Nearly every reusable item can be given.)
- Woodland Trust: www.woodlandtrust.org.uk/get-involved schools/green-tree-school-award/recycle/ (This charity runs a useful service for recycling Christmas cards.)
- Cancer Research: www.cancerresearchuk.org/support-us/donate/donate-goods (This charity has over 500 shops and will sell on most items.)

iii. Other organisations

Once you have your own recycling taken care of then you can think about approaching local businesses and other community members to see if they will recycle their used items for your benefit. Most will be only too happy to help.

In fact, this kind of request is a particularly good one to make to local businesses that do not know you. Such firms are very unlikely to give you money immediately. Instead requests like recycling are easy and inexpensive to meet and so make a good way to initiate a relationship. A little further along the line you can always go back and ask for money!

Payroll Giving

Approximately 2% of the population give to good causes via Payroll Giving. The reason that the figure is so low is largely down to a lack of awareness of the benefits. However, once signed up many donors and employers continue indefinitely. Given that such income is unrestricted (i.e. can be spent on anything charitable), it is well worth schools taking advantage.

i. Why bother?

Giving to your school via Payroll Giving is perhaps the most efficient way to do so for most working people. In effect, every £1 given to your school costs the donor:

- 80p if they are a lower rate taxpayer
- 60p if they are a higher rate taxpayer
- 55p if they are an additional rate taxpayer

So ask yourself: if you were a taxpayer would you rather give £1 at the school gate or £1 from your monthly pay?

ii. How to set up

In order to be able to benefit from Payroll Giving, you will need your donors to ask their employers to sign up with an approved Payroll Giving Agency (see www.gov.uk/government/publications/payroll-giving-approved-agencies/list-of-approved-payroll-giving-agencies for a list).

Most employers will be happy to sign up. However, where there is a reluctance, you might wish to provide a letter from the head teacher explaining why the school is seeking funds and why this is an important part of the process. You could also explain the benefits of Payroll Giving to employers, in particular in keeping staff happy. The donor can then give the letter to his or her employer.

If the company is already signed up with a Payroll Giving agency, or does so by means of the above, then your donor need only fill in one form detailing how much he or she would like to give your school charity. (The Payroll Giving agency will provide the employer with these details.)

If you are not registered as a charity then speak with Schools Funding Network (www.schoolsfundingnetwork.co.uk) which can act as an intermediary in such circumstances.

iii. Costs

Depending on the agency used, costs can be minimal (as little as 25p per donor per month). The costs are taken from the donor's gross pay, along with the donation, usually every month. As a school, there are no costs incurred at all.

iv. Leveraging donations
You could try and make such donations go further by asking relevant employers to:

- Pay the administration charge (which qualifies as a tax-allowable expense)
- Match the employee's monthly donation.

In such a way, you are benefiting from monthly donations from the donor and the employer.

v. Payroll Giving in your school
Of course, the school itself could sign up to a Payroll Giving agency. In that way, paid staff could give to the school tax-effectively too. If that sounds a bit too much to expect of school staff, you can always explain that they could give to another charity instead!

Major donor fundraising
Major donors are individuals that can make a 'transformative' impact to your school. Whatever your school's size, position or background, it is likely that there will be a pool of potential major donors who would give to you.

Raising funds from such donors is best approached by following a 7-step approach:

1. Identify
2. Research
3. Plan
4. Involve
5. Ask
6. Close
7. Thank

These stages will be explained below.

1. Identify
This is the stage where you build up a list of possible prospects to approach. Many of the tasks are similar to the process outlined for general funding in Chapter 6, with some additional nuances.

When looking for prospects, you are looking for anybody who has the capacity to give a large sum. In essence, these will be rich individuals with disposable income. The latter point is important – there are a good many people who are asset-rich but cash-poor and while their houses might be worth a huge amount they will feel unable to give you much at all.

Cast your net wide and far! The following are all potential targets:

- Friends and family members
- Local business people
- Any trustees of grant-making trusts
- Anybody showing an interest in the school
- School suppliers
- Parents
- Alumni
- Local residents
- Business associates of your school community, for instance parents who work with rich individuals.

In order to determine specific individuals within those broad groups, you might try any of the following:

- Speak to staff – staff members, particularly those who have been at the school for a long time, can often provide useful pointers to rich parents and alumni, as well as to those who have given in the past.
- Governors – chairs of governors in particular can often advise on who has given large sums.
- Speak to parents – sizing each other up is perhaps something parents inevitably do. Those showing signs of having large disposable funds will usually be quickly identified.
- Speak to alumni (more appropriate at secondary level) – like parents, alumni often keep tabs on each other and keep a metaphorical score of how well they are doing against each other. You can be fairly sure that at least a few of the school's ex-pupils are aware of anyone who has done extremely well.
- Follow local news items – local newspapers and news programmes often name successful individuals in the area.

As you go along, you should be building a database of information. Over time this will become your first source of potential donors. Items that you might care to record and which point to potential largesse include:

- Past donations – naturally, the higher the better.
- Addresses – websites such as Zoopla (www.zoopla.co.uk) give an estimate of the value of property related to particular postcodes, helping you gain an overview of overall wealth.
- Payments – cheques or payments made from private banks are a sure sign of wealth as there are normally minimum income thresholds that need to be met before someone can join.
- Occupations – keeping a note of occupations of parents and alumni can often pinpoint wealth. This can also be helpful where you are looking for in-kind voluntary support.
- Email addresses – these can provide pointers as to where people work as the organisational name is usually included in a work email. Again, this can help identify your well-paid stakeholders or provide a route into organisations which would otherwise be inaccessible without an inside contact.
- Titles – this need not only concern peers of the realm. For instance, 'Dr' Gupta suggests a certain income level.

Wealth screening – if you have a large enough database then you could consider using a wealth screening firm. This will do a lot of the above work for you as well as cross-check your list against a pre-established one of known rich and influential people. Some reputable wealth screening firms are listed in the Resources section on page 150.

As you identify people, make a rough estimate of how much they might be able to give. This should be done quickly – you can undertake more detailed analysis once you have decided that the prospect is worthy of being pursued.

2. Research

This stage is concerned with reducing the prospects found in stage 1 into a manageable and prioritised list. To do this you will be rating your prospects by their estimated capacity to give and their interest in your school.

- **Giving capacity**
  You should have a rough idea of net wealth from the Identify stage. If you have time and resource then you can refine your first estimate of expected wealth by working through house prices, estimated salary, shareholdings, directorships, past charitable donations etc. Use sites such as Companies House, Zoopla, LinkedIn and Google to glean specific information. However, do not go overboard on research – knowing that someone is worth £1.13m is not much more useful than knowing that they are worth £1m. Instead, simply aim to be confident that a prospect is in the optimum gift range (see below). Once you have calculated gift capacity, your aim is to link each prospect to a giving band, such as the following:

  1. £1,000-£4,999
  2. £5,000-£9,999
  3. £10,000-£24,999
  4. £25,000-£49,999
  5. £50,000-£99,999
  6. £100,000+

  To help you determine potential gift capacity and which level is correct, you can use the following guidelines and rules of thumb:

  1. Previous gifts to you and other charities
  2. 1% of net wealth
  3. 5% of current annual income

  Naturally, as you get to know your major donors in greater detail, you will be able to confirm or amend your giving bands accordingly.

- **Interest**
  Of course, wealth is no guarantee that funds will come your way. Instead, you need to determine how warmly the prospect views your school. Here is one way that you might go about rating your prospects:

  1. Cold – no engagement with the school and interests unknown.
  2. Lukewarm – no engagement with the school but known interest in the theme of the fundraising.

3. Lapsed funder – previous supporter of the school, likely to re-engage if involved.
4. Warm – some interaction with the school or close to a school stakeholder. For instance a parent.
5. Active – engaged with the school.
6. Involved – driving the school forward. For instance a school governor.

Once you have undertaken the two aspects, you can then prioritise your prospects by aggregating the giving capacity score and the interest as per the table below:

Gift	Giving Capacity	Interest	Priority Rating
Mr and Mrs J. Wells	3	4	7
Lily Chang	2	4	6
C. Connolly	1	6	7
P. Patel	4	5	9
George Grossmith	3	3	6

Table 4 Prioritised prospect list

In the above example, C. Connolly has the most interest in giving to the school but little capacity to give – better to approach P. Patel who has a higher overall priority rating.

3. Plan

Once you have your prioritised prospect list, you should create a strategy of engagement with your top potential donors. Points to consider include:

Donor motivation: social donors will need events and platforms where they can be seen; giving out the prizes at sports day might be one such opportunity you provide. *Philanthropic* donors will want to see how funding you will benefit the whole community; inviting such prospects to meetings where members of the local community are discussing your plans could be helpful. *Affinity* donors will want to see your school do well; inviting such donors to events or competitions where members of your school are achieving great things will inspire such people. *Mutual benefit* donors will want something in return; inviting such people to meet companies already supporting your school is one way to show such people that you are aware and comfortable with commercial realities.

Timescale: consider how long it might take to engage your prospects. Someone who is low on interest but has a high capacity to give will require more work than someone who is high on interest but low on capacity to give. While both prospects might have been classed as having the same level of attractiveness as a fundraising target, you will need to create more engagement opportunities for the former.

Try to have a minimum of two engagement activities for each prospect so that you always have a follow-on activity to offer when you meet a donor. Of course, plans will change as you spend more time with donors – a donor you had classed as being philanthropic might turn out to be equally motivated by the social angle; your plans will need to adapt accordingly.

4. Involve

This is the stage where you seek to increasingly engage and inspire your prospects. Every engagement you have with the major donor should be aimed at making the donation more likely. What this amounts to in practice is:

Vision: you should be creating a more and more graphic picture in the donor's mind of how their donation would make a difference. This vision should become increasingly well-defined as you get to know your prospect better.

Objections: Identifying and overcoming objections is really what this stage is about. The major donor might have twenty or so reasons why he or she does not want to give to you at present, some of them unconscious. You need to unearth these and provide convincing reasons why these are not in fact real issues. For instance, if someone says that they do not have the funds in one year, then perhaps they could pledge a gift for the following year so that you can at least start planning for the donation.

Win-wins: It can be a fine balancing act to ensure that both the needs of the donor and the school will both be met when a donation eventually comes. Generally the richer and bigger the major donor, the more likely you are to be faced with demands and suggestions that take you outside the original school plans. Careful negotiation of these conflicting demands will need to be undertaken – you do not want to lose all sight of the school's aims, yet on the other hand if you are too inflexible the donor will go somewhere else. This area is really an art rather than a science and you will need to determine the best course of action as you go along.

Timing: This step can prove to be a very long process, sometimes taking years. However, the biggest mistake most fundraisers make is not asking for a donation. If you think a major donor is ready to be asked but are not entirely sure then ask an open question initially, such as 'Would you like to support in some way?'. If the answer is negative then you have not caused any harm and can simply continue building the relationship. If the answer is positive then you can move on to more specific questions.

5. Ask

Well done if you reach this step! It is tempting to put this stage off as no one likes a rejection but this is the point to which the previous stages have been leading.

Amount: Very rarely ask for a direct sum. Rather ask open questions and make suggestions. For instance, 'One donor gave a six-figure sum last year. Would you be comfortable at that level?' Alternatively, show them your Gift Table (i.e. the various gifts that you will need to raise if you are to hit your target, such as one donor at £50,000, two donors at £20,000 etc.[8]) and ask them where they see themselves fitting in. Whatever you do, don't go in too low – major donors will very rarely say 'Actually, I'd be quite happy to give a lot more than your suggested figure'!

Objections: Reasons might still be thrown up by the major donor as to why he or she cannot give at this stage. Answer these as best you can as they can often be overcome. Major donors who are new to giving, who have not given to you before, or who are giving a larger amount than they ever have before, will very likely raise one or two objections when you ask.

Pregnant pauses: There is often a silence when the major donor is asked to make a gift. This can be very uncomfortable for both parties. Considering

---

[8] See the Marketing Plan section of Annual Campaigns on page 133 for more information on Gift Tables.

that it is you that has caused the discomfort, you will instinctively feel a desire to punctuate the silence and reduce the tension. This is not a good idea! Instead, allow the major donor to work through any issues or objections in his or her head. The fact that you are staying quiet and calm will reassure the donor that the relationship is still strong and that the request is reasonable and feasible.

Celebration: Once a decision to give has been made, you should look to end the business proceedings as quickly as possible. Simply agree a time to follow up with the particular details and then lift the atmosphere. You might want to show the donor round the school, pop by the head teacher's office or visit the beneficiary project directly. The major donor should be picturing the change which his or her money will effect and be basking in the gratitude of the school and beneficiaries.

6. Close

This is when the practicalities and details of the donation will be worked out. Generally, it should not be done at the same time as the Ask.

Content: Summarise what you agreed last time and check that this is still all in order. Run through various details, such as:

- The timing of the gift, including any instalments.
- Tax implications, such as Gift Aid.
- Recognition, which is particularly important for donors with a social motivation.

Personnel: If you have secured a large sum, you might wish to bring an accountant or business manager with you. If you feel that your relationship with the major donor might be knocked as you work out particular details then you could delegate this part to someone else. This can be particularly true when someone is covering the costs of a project and there might be a discussion of the budget.

7. Thank

This is where you renew feelings of motivation in the major donor following the rather dry Closing stage above.

Amount: While it may be tempting to have all and sundry thank the

donor, particularly for large gifts, you should keep one or two people in reserve who can then inject more energy into a follow-up request.
Tangible benefits: If you have agreed certain benefits then you will need to deliver on these. For instance, naming rights to buildings or classrooms should be followed up.

Next gift: You should already be planning a new series of engagement activities with the donor. In other words, go back to Stage 3!

Measurement and Review
As you build your database, you should keep track of the stage at which each of your major donor prospects sits. What you will often find is that certain donors get stuck at particular stages or that the school is struggling at a particular step, such as finding prospects or closing negotiations. Once that area is identified, you can begin to brainstorm tactics for improving the weakness. As time goes by, you will become better and better at raising large sums.

Company fundraising

Raising support from companies (also known as corporate fundraising) requires a somewhat different approach to purely philanthropic fundraising. The key points to take into account when seeking such support are discussed below.

i. Why do companies give?
Companies give support for a number of reasons, including:

- The desire to build goodwill and a positive public image
- To increase revenues
- To increase customer numbers
- For tax benefits
- To attract, motivate and retain employees
- To improve the communities in which they operate
- To support causes championed by the Chairman or CEO.

ii. What support can I seek from a company?
Companies give in a number of ways. The most successful school-company relationships will incorporate several approaches.

8. The fundraising disciplines

- Staff time

Large organisations often have formal volunteering programmes where, for instance, staff might be given three paid days off for volunteering activities. Smaller firms, although lacking the time and resource to undertake large-scale volunteering, are often closely connected to their local communities and therefore more inclined to offer support where possible.

Remember to fully recognise such time given – it might well have cost the company several hundred pounds for each volunteer offered.

- In-kind support

Products, training and services all fall into this category. There is usually a self-enlightened angle to such support in that companies are hoping that beneficiaries will be so impressed by the support that they will either become future customers or will recommend others. This shouldn't cause you to devalue the gift – most companies are aware that the gift needs to be worth something in its own right.

- Cash donations

Companies will give cash, but usually after they have given non-cash support first and built a relationship with you. A number of larger companies have their own foundations and these are largely independent of the profit-making company – in effect, they work just like charitable foundations. Small and medium-sized enterprises (SMEs), which make up the bulk of UK companies, are unlikely to have such formal arrangements – support is usually decided by the head of the company.

- Cause related marketing (CRM)

CRM occurs when a company makes a donation to a particular cause or organisation every time a sale of a product or service takes place. For instance, a local travel agent could run a campaign along the lines of '5% of any purchase is given to Greenacres School'. The business attracts more customers and the school receives funds. If you enter into any CRM relationship, ensure that the company's brand fits your school's ethos. See the section on Cause related marketing on page 83 for more details.

iii. What should I include in a proposal?
Large companies will almost certainly have guidelines for submissions. For

other organisations, it is nearly always worth speaking to a decision-maker before writing so that you are clear on what would be most helpful.

Whether speaking or writing to a company, you should:

- Be clear why it is in the company's interest to support (see the Why do companies give? section above). This should be apparent almost from the very first sentence of any communication to maintain the company's interest.
- Be able to describe what support you are seeking succinctly and why it is needed.
- Be confident that what you are requesting is something that is within the company's capacity to give.

If you are asked to send in a proposal and there are no rules or advice on the formatting, simply follow the guidelines for a standard proposal set out in the section on Trust and statutory applications (page 56 *et seq*). That format suits companies just as much as trusts, with one major exception: break the Benefits section into two, so that you have the following headings:

- Summary (including the key benefits for the company)
- Background
- The project
- Budget
- Benefits to company
- Benefits to school
- Conclusion.

iv. How much should I ask for?

There are normally two types of budget you can tap into when dealing with companies: a marketing or commercial one, and a philanthropic one. The former budget is invariably larger than the latter, though you will need to work harder to access it.

Marketing/Corporate budget

Most companies are motivated by the *mutual benefit* motivation so will be weighing up the value that any partnership brings them in return for their support. As a consequence, aim to make the benefits derived from any partnership roughly equal in value – if one side does much better than the other then the relationship will likely break down. In other words, if you are seeking £5,000 from a business then you should be offering £5,000 of benefits in return. In such a way, the decision by the business to spend the money on you rather than on, for example, advertising in the local newspaper where it could also reach parents becomes a simple one. After all, all things being equal, the preference will be for your school because it is the more 'worthy' proposition.

Philanthropic budget
Remember that any company making a cash donation to your school can offset the support against corporation tax (this is not the case where the business is getting a business benefit back in return). This is an important factor that is missed by a surprising number of companies and fundraisers alike! It means that a £10,000 donation will likely cost the company a good deal less than its nominal amount. So when asking for purely philanthropic donations from companies, ensure that you point out this tax incentive.

Exploiting school premises
If your school offers its facilities to hire then you can start bringing in income outside normal school hours as well as linking with your community.

i. What can be hired out?
Sport facilities, theatre or school halls, as well as meeting rooms are all items that local groups and communities will likely wish to use. In addition, you might wish to offer support staff or equipment to add further value to your proposition.

Bear in mind that there are risks in letting external people and groups into your premises, not least the potential for damage to facilities. You should run through these risks and plan how you would manage such problems if they were to occur, before proceeding.

There are also staffing issues that need to be addressed. For instance, do you have someone willing to keep your school open later than normal? If so, you should ensure that the income you receive exceeds any associated costs with additional staffing.

ii. Marketing
Once you have decided what you are offering, you will need to work up a marketing proposition. This can be produced as a small brochure or simply appear on your website.

Pictures coupled with detailed descriptions should show off your facilities and times of availability should be given. You will need to do some market research on the pricing. For instance, if you are hiring out a football pitch, you will want to know how much it costs elsewhere in your community, pricing accordingly.

Once you have your publicity materials drawn up, you will need to promote it to the local community. While your newsletter and website will be good options for reaching your immediate school community, you should also think about promoting further afield. A door-drop, local advertising, and flyers given to local businesses and community groups are all potential options.

iii. Contracts

Unless the hiring value is very small, it is worth drawing up a standard contract modifiable for individual clients. In that way, you can protect yourself to some degree from any damage that may occur. You can also set minimum standards of behaviour and of course make clear your pricing.

iv. Outsourcing

There are a number of organisations, usually private firms, which have sprung up to cater for this area. Some specialise in marketing while others provide a complete service, including staffing. Try School Plus (www.schoolsplus.co.uk) or School Hire (www.schoolhire.co.uk).

Sponsorship

Sponsorship is a commercial relationship that results in funding being given to your school in return for the sponsor being able to associate itself with something belonging to you.

i. Things you could sponsor

Almost anything can be sponsored, as long as it provides visibility for the sponsor amongst its desired audience.

- Events
- Newsletters
- Sports teams
- Orchestras
- A building (even a front wall!)
- Your website.

ii. How much should we charge?

There is no easy answer to this, even though certain sponsorship firms attempt to dazzle potential clients with fancy formulas.

Minimum levels

Sponsorship is not straightforward and there is no point in undertaking it unless you can make a certain amount of money. So set a certain level which it would not be worth going below. To help you determine this number, work out all the hours that would be needed to achieve the sponsorship agreement and deliver on it. I suggest that you include an arbitrary rate for volunteers as there is no point in them working for the sponsor for nothing. Whatever that cost is, you want to at least double it and probably triple it to make sponsorship worthwhile.

Fair value

However, sponsorship is not just about covering costs. It is about extracting a fair payment in return for providing sponsor benefits. So in addition to your minimum level, you should take in the following factors:

- The market rate – if you sold your sponsorship rights for £5,000 and others were willing to offer £10,000 then you have missed out, however profitable the £5,000 might be. Speaking to a variety of potential sponsors as well as looking at other comparable sponsorship opportunities can all guide.
- The scarcity value – the fewer sponsorship opportunities that you offer then the more valuable such benefits will be to a sponsor.
- Time factors – the more time a sponsor has to 'leverage' its sponsorship (e.g. by building sales campaigns around it) the more valuable it will be to a sponsor. Ideally, you would be looking to tie up a sponsor several months before an event or activity.
- Economic factors – sponsorship budgets are often one of the first things to be cut in times of economic difficulty so be prepared for sponsorship levels to go up and down in respect of the economic cycle.

iii. Contracts

Sponsorship arrangements should result in a contract, or a memorandum of understanding (MoU)[9] as a minimum. It is beyond the scope of this book to give sample contracts or MoUs but if you are not sure how to draw up such an agreement then it would be worth speaking to a local legal firm. With luck, they will offer to draw one up for you on a pro bono basis. Failing that, they will almost certainly be able to point you to information that will enable you to draw one up.

Text giving

For people who are short of time, constantly on the go and subject to lots of demands, text giving is an excellent way to support good causes, so could be an ideal option for parents. In addition, younger people are quick to take up new technologies and will generally prefer these electronic means of giving than the traditional ones (as a result, they are good for alumni). In fact, text giving is growing rapidly so it might certainly be worth giving it a trial.

i. Providers

The first thing to do is find a provider. JustTextGiving (www.vodafone.co.uk/about-us/just-text-giving/) or instagiv (instagiv.com) are two well-known providers. (You will need to have a charity number in order to register. Contact Schools Funding Network if this is a problem as they might be willing to front a charitable campaign for you (www.schoolsfundingnetwork.co.uk).

ii. Fundraising by text

Once you are registered with a provider, the general principles of fundraising apply, that is you need to explain clearly why someone should give to you and publicise the fact that this means of giving is available to your donor base.

Being concise is doubly important and your calls to action must be clear and sharp. If you ever travel by train or tube, you will have a good chance to see examples of the campaigns used by the big charities. Try and copy their styles as they will have tested what works and what does not.

Where might you promote the service? An obvious one is at the school gates – parents milling around waiting to pick up their children offer an

---

[9] While not enforceable in law, unlike contracts, MoUs can be useful in avoiding confusion or misunderstandings and are probably the best option for most schools dealing with projects under £50,000.

excellent opportunity for a quick spur-of-the-moment donation to be made. Similarly, if your school uses any of the group messaging services then this is a good way to get the message out.

iii. Monitoring

Keep an eye on the amount of support you are raising via texts. If you find that a good many people are giving this way then it will be worth putting a greater emphasis on this form of giving. If only a few people are involved then consider dropping the option or at least not spending too much time or resource on promoting it.

While text giving is unlikely to be a game-changer for your school, the proportion of your total funds raised in this way will likely increase as time goes by – technology is becoming ever more integrated into our lives. Certainly this is an area to keep an eye on!

Legacies

7% of people leave money to good causes in their Wills. Yet 35% say that they would be happy to leave a legacy to such causes once their friends and families were provided for, potentially providing an extra £7 billion each year. As a consequence, if you can meet this requirement (namely, enable people to care for their loved ones and inspire them in your school) you can unlock potentially very large sums.

i. Types of legacy

There are two main types of legacy for the purposes of school fundraising:

Pecuniary legacies

These occur when a set sum is given, such as £1,000. There are some disadvantages in this type of legacy. For instance, if the pledge is given many years before the legacy is paid out then inflation will most likely have eaten up a significant amount of the value of the gift. In addition, particularly if the donation is large, a pecuniary legacy can cause resentment amongst family members if they feel it is too large in proportion to their share.

Residual legacies

These occur when the amount that is given is only paid out once specific sums have been distributed to family and friends and all debts have been discharged. In other words, it caters for the 35% of people who say that they would leave money to a good cause once their friends and family are taken care of.

For example, if 25% of a residual legacy was left to your school and there was £20,000 left after friends and family plus debts had been paid then you would receive £5,000.

As well as being much more palatable to family members, this method of leaving money does not suffer from the inflationary issue of pecuniary legacies.

ii. Marketing

Once you decide that legacy fundraising is something that you wish to promote then you will need to let potential legators know that leaving something to your school is both possible and welcome. That means taking account of several factors:

Tone

It is essential that you keep the tone positive and bright. So make no specific mention of death or other morbid terms. That even includes the term 'legacy' – much better to use words like 'gift' or slightly better 'legacy gift'.

Instead you want to be portraying a picture of how your school will develop and flourish over the long-term thanks to gifts in Wills. You should do this by giving a clear vision of the future and how a legacy will help cement the school's position. Try not to be too pushy. What you are aiming to do is make people aware that they should consider their legacies, with the school being one potential beneficiary once friends and family are looked after.

Messaging

You should be using as many opportunities as possible to promote your wish to receive income from legacies, not least because it requires a drip-feed approach to get the message across before people act.

Keep your messaging simple and clear and try and cover these areas:
- An overarching message, such as, 'Any gift, however small, left in your Will makes a difference to our school'
- Make clear that the person leaving the gift should ensure friends and family are looked after first
- Explain your vision for the school over the following decades (not your immediate needs!)

- Explain how to go about leaving the gift, in the main this being speaking to a solicitor.

One area which is best avoided is 'pledge stories'. These occur when someone explains how they left a gift and suggests that others do the same. They are off-putting and will rarely result in support.

Publicity vehicles

Perhaps the best way to promote the giving of legacies is in your newsletter. It is a non-intrusive way of showing that such gifts can create a bright future for your school. As a consequence, you should consider including at least one piece on this area every time you send out a newsletter. In such a way, the idea of leaving something to the school in one's Will becomes normalised and you will begin to build up your legacy pledges and income.

Events are also a good way to promote legacies. These can be run subtly, such as special events for anyone who has made a legacy pledge. As well as giving you the opportunity to thank this group of people, the publicity will show others that this is a valuable area for you.

You could also arrange an event with a solicitor who could run through the importance of making a Will and how to go about it. These have been popular with large charities, not least because there are millions of people who have not made a Will.

Another means of publicising this form of giving is by undertaking a direct mail piece, showing potential supporters how they can support the school in their Wills.

One area which is surprisingly ineffective and indeed potentially harmful is the telephone. Being called to discuss legacies seems to put people off and is seen as too grasping.

Who to target

Overall, you will want to target all the stakeholders in the school that you have identified, giving particular attention to those coming up to retirement age and beyond, though remembering that it is rarely ever too soon to make a Will!

Endowment funds

Legacies combine very well with endowment funds, both running over many years. You can combine marketing efforts for both by linking the two together. For instance, if you have an endowment for future building needs that runs over the next 15 years then you might explain that legacies constitute one way that the endowment can be built up. (See the Endowments section starting on page 143 for more details on this form of fundraising.)

iii. Updates
An annual update of the school's progress, along with the school's newsletter, is all that is needed for those who have pledged a gift in their Wills. Legators want to feel they are part of an institution that is going to be around for a long time – they don't want to be reminded of their mortality so rarely need special updates.

iv. Measurements
One downside of legacies is that pledges often fail to materialise. In fact, experts in the field recommend that the only items worth measuring are legacies that materialise, as well as the number of legacy communications put out. So while you may be initially elated when someone says that they will leave you £50,000 in their Will, privately you should only be joyous when you receive the money!

v. Benchmarking
It is worth looking at how the big charities go about legacies, as well as some of the leading private schools. Some are done very well, such as Cancer Research UK or Rugby School.

Cause related marketing
Cause related marketing (CRM) is a technique that can be used to raise funds for your school from local businesses. The principle can be extended to other areas as well, for instance by incentivising school staff or indeed pupils.

i. CRM and local businesses
CRM involves a business making a donation to a specified good cause every time a certain action takes place. For instance, for every plant bought by a customer, 25p goes to the local school. The business advances its marketing goals (such as increasing sales or attracting new customers) while also advancing the good cause.

Businesses like to contribute and support their local schools but are reluctant to give money. This is usually because most local businesses will be small or because they have their own growth targets which need investment. As CRM enables the business to advance its own interests while simultaneously helping, any school which suggests this type of giving is likely to be better received and to be able to access larger sums.

Examples
It is worth suggesting CRM to companies in two main ways: external CRM and internal CRM. The former generally support the business's main operations, such as increasing sales, the latter supports behind-the-scenes activities, such as reducing absenteeism or staff turnover. Examples include:

External
- £25 to the school every time the local garage undertakes an MoT
- 5% of the sale price of certain items at the local furniture shop to the local school.

Internal
- £100 to the school for every member of staff who has a 100% attendance record over a 6 month period
- £1000 to the school reduced by £1 every time an employee is late.

ii. How to broker
For CRM to work well, you need to know what the organisation's business objectives are before you make any suggestions. So simply ask! For example, if the business is looking to launch a new product you could set up a CRM initiative that paid your school every time the new product was sold. If the goal is to retain existing clients, you could suggest a payment to the school every time there is a renewal.

Similarly, with internal CRM initiatives, simply ask the organisation if they have any issues with lateness or absenteeism. Such issues are almost universal to some degree so it is unlikely that you will meet a straight 'no'. Having a solution which helps both parties will be something the business is unlikely to expect but willing to try.

iii. Pricing
Give some thought to the value you bring. If the profit margin on a

particular item sold is £1 then the amount you can ask for of any sale is going to be small. However, if it is a question of an estate agent selling a house, the margins will be much larger. Similarly when incentivising internal actions, even cutting one day of absenteeism is likely to be worth £100 and upwards to the business simply on the lost wages being made up, so asking for anywhere from £25 to £50 is not unreasonable in this instance.

You might wish to consider minimum income guarantees on external CRM initiatives as well (i.e. you get paid a certain amount even if the company sells no products). This is because you are effectively lending the school's name to the company to use; you are not sharing the risk on a sales venture. Setting a level of a minimum income guarantee is tricky and depends on a number of commercial considerations (e.g. projected sales, profit margins, reputation of the company etc.). So only suggest them with bigger organisations or those where you feel the added guarantee is needed.

If both you and the business are happy with the outcomes and the rates then your pricing is a good one. If you feel exploited, or the business does, the relationship will soon fail – so above all, seek the win-win option.

iv. Ethical guidance

Ethical considerations are doubly important when raising support from companies. So consider with whom you might find it unacceptable to work. Having a written policy is useful if you have multiple people approaching potential partners or where there are likely to be conflicting views on such matters (see Ethical considerations on page 27).

v. Other things to mention

Of course, the hardest part in seeking support from companies is simply meeting the right people. So when you find yourself with the opportunity to discuss CRM, make sure you discuss the other support options, such as:

- Sponsorship of an event
- Payroll Giving
- Employee match-giving programmes (usually only big companies)
- Gift-in-kind donations
- One-off donations
- Staff volunteering.

Above all, look to build a relationship with the business, make it multi-faceted and ensure that both sides benefit.

vi. Alternatives to businesses

CRM need not only be used with businesses. For instance, you could try the following:
- Internal CRM initiatives within the school
- Within the PTA
- Amongst Governors – for instance a 'fine' for not turning up to a Governors' meeting!

Chapter 8 in a nutshell

This chapter forms the heart of the book, examining in detail each of the different options for raising support for the school that were first outlined in Chapter 5.

Each section in the chapter comprises a complete practical 'how to' guide for the fundraising method in question.

9
THE CASE FOR SUPPORT

The Case for Support, sometimes called the Case Statement, provides the background for everything a potential donor might want to know about your school. It is used to bring on advocates and volunteers, motivates existing staff, governors and supporters, and provides ready information for prospective grant applications and donor encounters.

In essence, a pre-written Case for Support makes unexpected funding opportunities much more manageable and creates a sense of purpose and direction to your fundraising.

Essential content

A meaningful document which will help your fundraising efforts should cover the following:

Future direction

Story-telling is a key part of fundraising and funders are looking to buy into interesting and credible stories. So where are you trying to take your school? What evidence is there of progress in this already? What will the future look like?

Virtually every funder wants to give to interesting and exciting projects which make a difference. So try and convey that sense of purpose and direction, making clear how the future can be made rosier with outside support.

Current objectives

What are your plans to achieve your vision of the future? If your goal is to be a centre of sporting excellence, then perhaps you are looking for state-of-the-art facilities, equipment and coaches? If it is to develop well-integrated and adapted members of society then perhaps you are looking for mentors and volunteers?

You should cover a variety of projects (three to five is about right) so that if a funder has no interest in, for example, sport they are not completely lost to you. You should include budgets, partly to show that you are not simply punting around for support, partly so that your fundraisers have an idea of how much funding is needed, and partly so that funders can properly assess how much they need to give to make a difference. In addition, show any support you have already raised – donors are much more likely to commit if there is a sign of others doing so as well.

Plan of action
Use this section to detail how you aim to meet your objectives and show potential supporters that you have given some proper thought to your goals. For instance, you might state that you are prioritising one project and will set aside budget for it, that you are delegating another to the PTA, and will only start work on a third one if a major donor comes forward.

Breaking large campaigns and targets down into more manageable sections will also help. For instance, '50% will come from selling naming rights to a local company, 30% from the school budget, 20% from charitable foundations.' That makes it more likely that those reading your Case for Support might be inspired to help out or suggest additional ways of meeting your goals.

Means of giving
The biggest mistake professional and non-professional fundraisers make is not asking for support (as has been mentioned elsewhere!) So use this section to show clearly how someone can give to you; provide contact details, including a named person.

Give some example donations, showing the difference that such a sum would make, for instance: '£10 would provide a mouse for our IT suite, £100 would…..'. Mention any benefits you would offer in return, for example, 'Donors giving £5,000 or more join our Gold Club, where they gain….'.

A comprehensive document
Your Case for Support is the go-to document for all your fundraisers. Therefore the more that you can include relevant material in an easily accessible fashion the better. Types of additional information that you might look to add include:

- Your ethical policy, i.e. guidance on what support is acceptable
- Standard proposals that can either be sent as they are or tailored for individual prospects
- Details of all major donors, including any particular stewardship plans
- Copies of past newsletters

- Website metrics
- Details of any community fundraisers working for you
- Subsections focused on particular fundraising activities, e.g. all the historical data and intelligence related to events, raffles and so on.
- Your thank you policy, so that any fundraiser can immediately see what benefits a gift of, say, £5,000 would bring a donor
- Your annual communication plan
- Your stewardship plan
- Details of Annual Campaigns, Capital Appeals or Endowments.

A work in progress

The Case for Support is a working document and should be updated from time to time. It should be made readily available to staff, your PTA and anyone else who might fundraise for you. Not only does this provide your 'workers' with the necessary information needed to raise support, it also provides them with a means of feeding back intelligence from their fundraising endeavours. For instance, knowing that 'Company A will provide 50% of the funding if the school can raise the rest' could well unlock a large donation from someone else – as long as all your fundraisers know that intelligence!

When everyone knows what you are seeking to do, along with the arguments and details for why and how support should be given, then you are much more likely to achieve your goals, and on time. Perhaps most satisfyingly, you will find that those chance meetings with potential supporters become much more likely and, with a little effort, common.

Chapter 9 in a nutshell

A written Case for Support is the most important document in any fundraising drive, having a variety of functions for different stakeholders.

The chapter explains the content, purpose and range of the Case for Support document, as well as the way in which the document will grow and develop as the fundraising programme progresses.

10
FUNDRAISING TOOLS TO GIVE YOU AN EDGE

This chapter details a variety of techniques that will help your fundraising. While you will no doubt be able to raise a reasonable amount of funds without them, by adding these tools to your armoury you will elevate your fundraising from the good to the sublime.

We will cover the following areas:

- Gift Aid
- 30-second pitch
- Match-giving
- Crowdfunding
- Listening and questioning
- Social media overview
- Facebook
- Twitter
- Stand-out features
- Storytelling
- Psychology of influence.

Gift Aid

Gift Aid enables you to claim an extra 25% on charitable donations made by UK tax-payers.[10] Your school should be taking advantage of it! Indeed, when the National Audit Office last looked at this area, it found that over £2 billion of donations that could have had Gift Aid claimed on them were not in fact 'gift-aided'. That is a lot of money being lost every year.

i. Claim immediately without charity or HMRC registrations

If your school is not currently claiming Gift Aid then perhaps the simplest solution is provided by The Funding Exchange. This is a charity which has been set up to support fundraising amongst schools and charities. It runs Schools Funding Network (www.schoolsfundingnetwork.co.uk) where schools can sign up to be members.

As part of this membership, schools can gain access to the charity's Gift Aid Recovery System. This removes all the difficulties of Gift Aid as

---

[10] For the tax relief arrangement in Ireland, see *CHY3 - Scheme of Tax Relief for Donations of Money or Designated Securities to 'Eligible Charities' and other 'Approved Bodies'* Under Section 848A Taxes Consolidation Act 1997 at www.revenue.ie/en/personal/charities.html

they put claims through their own Gift Aid registration. In other words, you do not need to have a charity number, register with HMRC or keep any paperwork.

They can also support campaigns on fundraising platforms outside their own, such as JustGiving. The turn-around is very quick so you can start benefiting from this tax benefit within 24 hours.

ii. Claiming through your own Gift Aid number

If you want to put through your own claims or have an agent do so for you then you will need to register with HMRC. You can do this at www.gov.uk/charity-recognition-hmrc.

Once registered, you will need to ensure that you comply with HMRC regulations and keep up with Gift Aid legislation.

30-second pitch

I am in a lift with you and ask politely what you do. Are you able to explain your fundraising brief and gain my interest in the brief time we have together? If you can, well done! You clearly have a 'lift pitch' already worked out. If not, you will benefit greatly by producing one.

i. Purpose

The 30-second pitch or lift pitch serves three purposes:

- It widens your list of prospects by allowing you to engage people who unexpectedly come across your radar (such as in lifts!)
- It enables you to engage busy people, who only have a small amount of time and want to work out quickly whether it is worth speaking with you.
- It enables those with whom you have spoken to pass on your needs clearly and concisely, such as a subordinate to their boss.
- It enables you to increase the number of people fundraising for your school, without them all having to take on lots of information.

ii. Producing your pitch

To produce the content of your 30-second pitch (1 minute if you're lucky), you need to provide answers to the following questions:

- What organisation do you represent?
- What is the problem you are trying to overcome?

- What is the solution?
- Why should I help you?

For example, if you were trawling for raffle prizes then you might come up with a lift pitch such as the following:

'I am from Horizons Academy. We have some very talented musicians and are looking to buy a grand piano so that our children can practice on a first-class instrument. I am looking for prizes that might be raffled to raise the necessary funds. If you gave something, you would help us in our goal while lots of our parents and staff would think what a wonderful business your company was. Here's my card / flyer – if you or anyone else would like to become involved then do drop me a line.'

iii. Increasing your fundraising workforce

Your lift pitch will become more effective the more people use it. That does not mean that the exact same wording needs to be used by everybody – the delivery must come across as authentic and will be unique to each individual. However, the three main steps (i.e. the problem, solution and benefit) will be the same and should be shared freely and widely with anyone who could raise funds for you.

Match-giving

Match-funding is an incredibly powerful technique to unlock support. For instance, research conducted by Dr Catherine Walker on behalf of The Big Give found that 84% of respondents were more likely to give if there was matching, while donations given in a sample were 2.5 times higher with such a mechanism. As a result, why not take advantage of this phenomenon by creating your own match-funds or challenges?

i. More effective funding requests

Here is a typical fundraising request by a school:

'We are trying to raise £10,000 for new musical instruments. Please give generously'.

Now compare it with this one:

'We are trying to raise £10,000 for new musical instruments. Mr and Mrs

Smith will match any donations on a £1-to-£1 up to a maximum of £5,000. Please give generously'.

The latter request is much more powerful and will be all the more successful as a result.

ii. Setting up match-challenges

Here is a quick way to set up this type of fundraising request:

Approach a funder with the capacity to give the challenge target

Businesses are often a good target because they gain a lot of publicity in the process. However, any big funder is a possibility – the positive psychological effect of unlocking someone else's funds works whether it is the challenger unlocking lots of little funds or the smaller donors unlocking one donor's large pot.

Set the challenge and give a deadline

For example, 'ABC Garden Centre will match any donations raised between now and June up to a maximum amount of £5,000'.

Approach smaller donors

Ask parents and other smaller funders for help in meeting the challenge. You should present this as a potential loss to take advantage of the psychological effect that human beings react more strongly to losses than to gains[11]. So, for example, please help us raise £5,000 for our new landscaping so that we don't lose £5,000 from ABC Garden Centre'.

Keep your small donors up-to-date with progress

Some small donors will only give at certain stages, such as when they feel that the target is near to completion. So give continuous updates.

Involve big donors if need be

If your smaller funders look unlikely to hit the target without a huge effort, consider approaching one of your bigger funders. While they are better for setting such challenges, you do not want to lose potential income. And, failing that, you might always ask the challenge-setter to give you any funding not unlocked as a gesture of goodwill if you fail.

---

[11] One study found that the average person would prefer to avoid a £100 loss rather than gain £200. Not logical but worth knowing!

Crowdfunding

There are various websites which now cater for crowdfunding. These originated in the venture capital industry and have now extended into the charity and fundraising arenas.

i. Definition

In essence, crowdfunding is where you set a target which is then reached via lots of small online donations. A deadline is given to create a sense of urgency to the campaign.

Some crowdfunding sites have an option of giving small donors something back in return for giving. In addition, some sites return funds to donors if the target has not been reached in time. The sites themselves make money by taking a percentage of any funds raised.

ii. Running a crowdfunding campaign

When setting the target, make sure it is a realistic one. If you have to raise £25,000 in four weeks, it is very unlikely that you will be able to do so via online donations. In practice, potential donors will see the target and refuse to give, believing that a successful campaign is unachievable.

Where you are giving something in return for donations, ensure that it is not too onerous for you to deliver. For instance, offering a free raffle ticket for every £10 donation would be relatively simple. If you do go down this route, make sure your gifts do not fall foul of the Gift Aid rules. At the time of writing, you can give benefits to donors at the following levels:

Donations	Maximum value of benefit
up to £100	25% of the donation
£101 - £1000	£25
£1,001 and over	5% of the donation (up to £2,500)

Make sure the crowdfunding site that you use caters for Gift Aid, as many do not. If you are missing out on Gift Aid, you are missing a big trick! (See page 92 for more on Gift Aid.)

Once you have set your target, put in place a deadline and decided whether to give any gift in return, you should make a concerted effort to alert your prospects. In general, these should be your smaller donors. For instance, you do not want to undermine a long-term approach to a major donor by asking for £50 for a crowdfunding campaign when a £50,000 request could be made a little later on.

Stress the urgency of the campaign and make clear any benefits you are giving in return. You should keep up a steady stream of communications throughout the campaign as some donors will need several requests before they get round to giving.

Overall, crowdfunding is a fun activity which appeals to certain types of donor, particularly the young. However, how much money you make from this type of fundraising is debatable, particularly in relation to the amount of effort expended.

Listening and questioning

In some ways, fundraising is like selling – you are selling a vision of your school to a prospective donor who will then give in return. As a result, some fundraisers, including very experienced ones, fall into the trap of believing that a fast sales patter is the way to achieve donations. It might work once or twice with small donations but if you are trying this approach with a large donor it is usually the 'kiss of death'.

The best way to gain a big donation is by intimately understanding the giving motivations of your donors. You do this by asking questions and listening intensely to the responses. You should be constantly checking that you have fully understood what the donor has said. For instance, a lot of major donors rarely give the real reason that they are reluctant to give until they have built up a good deal of trust and rapport with you. That only comes about when you show that you understand where the donor is coming from.

A rough rule of thumb I was given when starting off in major charities was 20% talking time against 80% listening. Of course, if you are in a set-piece arrangement, such as a formal pitch, then the amount of talking you do will go up. However, as a general guideline the 20%-80% split is a good one for most meetings. Indeed, if you have found yourself talking for a long time and have no idea whether the side opposite agrees, disagrees or is indifferent to what you have just said then you have not been asking enough questions or sufficiently listening!

Social media overview

Facebook, Twitter and other social media sites (the so-called Web 2.0) are all useful for engaging and inspiring donors. They are less useful when it comes to directly raising funds but if you have developed a strong social media presence then your actual fundraising should benefit considerably.

i. A suggested strategy

Social media is certainly flavour of the month. Yet it is such a broad sphere, it can often be difficult to know where to start. One way to break it down into manageable chunks is to build up your offering in three main stages as below:

Stage 1 – Essentials (Boosts your income)

These items are the traditional and oldest functions of the digital age (sometimes called by the catch-all 'Web 1.0'). You should have these items set up before you try anything else:

- Website
- Online donation facility (either directly on your website or with a link to an external provider)
- E-newsletter

Given their importance, these facilities have been given their own sections above in Chapter 8 (the online donation facility is incorporated into the Website section).

Stage 2 – Interaction (Boosts your supporter numbers)

The two key platforms for this stage are:

- Facebook
- Twitter

These sites increase interest and engagement, driving people to give through the facilities in Stage 1. They require ongoing staff or volunteer time, with 5,000 likes or followers often being seen as being the tipping point before meaningful results are seen. As a result, they take time before they become truly effective.

We will run through factors to take into account with Facebook and Twitter in the next two sections after this one.

Stage 3 – Nice-to-have

These are unlikely to make a huge difference to your overall totals. However, some people like them and if you want a comprehensive development outfit then you should look to include them:

- Flickr
- Blogs
- YouTube
- LinkedIn

If you are interested in learning more about these options, they are described in ample detail online, including in material put out by the providers themselves.

ii. General principles
Objectives
It is worth writing down your objectives from the start – without them, social media can hoover up time without any noticeable gain. So, for instance, you might note that you wish to increase website traffic by 10%, raise the number of online donations by 100, and increase the number of people subscribed to your newsletter by 200 over the next 6 months.

Next, write down the resources you are willing to invest in each activity. If you were undertaking a full range of social media activities outlined above, you would need the equivalent of a full-time person and probably more. That might be possible if split amongst various PTA members, but unlikely if simply added to staff's existing workloads.

Finally, come up with relevant measurements, such as Twitter followers, website traffic, online funds raised, newsletter subscribers, Facebook fans, volunteers and event attendees. Take a measurement every month.

General tips
- Choose an appropriate name which is the same for your website, Facebook, Twitter and YouTube accounts. Include geographical details if your name is one shared by a lot of schools. For instance, there are 170 schools called St Peter's Primary School so you need to ensure that people can readily find yours!
- Create a record of all passwords and login details and keep it in a safe place. Access should be limited to essential people.
- Set up a Google account, choosing a username that matches your other social media names. Having such an account allows you to set up YouTube and take advantage of services such as Google Analytics.
- Some IT skills, even basic HTML, can be useful in adding an extra

element to your social media. There is a good chance that amongst your school community you have an IT professional or budding future Bill Gates – use them!
- If your social media activity is advanced then consider using a social media dashboard, like HootSuite. This allows you to co-ordinate and schedule activity, gain detailed analytics as well as do a host of other things.
- Similarly, if you have a big outfit then you might wish to create a social media policy. That will include such items as precluding any negative comment about the school by official fundraisers.
- Follow large and respected organisations, which you would like to emulate. In particular, try to follow at least two other schools, two charities and two companies. In addition, you might consider following your leading American equivalents – they are often ahead of the UK and you can pick up a good many ideas this way.
- Create a powerful banner to go across all your social media and e-newsletter. That helps build your 'brand'.
- Keep building up follower numbers until you reach your watershed moment when this number seems to grow rapidly.
- Create a central hub where photos of events, activities and projects can be stored. These can be used to refresh your website, update Facebook, and keep engagement high. It is unlikely that you will want or need to buy copyrighted photos to complement your own. If you do need more photos, or pictures for a specific purpose, then try Google Images or Flickr where you can download pictures for free and safe from copyright issues.
- Do not use a third-party email domain name for your communications, such as Gmail or Yahoo. It smacks of amateurism and will limit your fundraising reach, particularly amongst larger donors.

Facebook

Facebook is used by hundreds of millions of people every day. As a means of raising awareness of your funding needs, there are few better means of doing so than using Facebook.

i. Getting started
- You can sign up to Facebook here: www.facebook.com/directory pages/
- You cannot change your Facebook Page name once you have set it

up so make sure it is right first time and tallies with your other social media platforms.
- Do not create a 'Cause' or 'Topic' page for your primary Facebook Page. They are better for separate campaigns.

ii. Content
- Try and create a 'voice', so that followers can identify with a real-life person behind the site.
- Add links, photos and video to your status updates so that they are more engaging. Facebook gives a lot of weight to these three elements in its algorithm, meaning that you will appear more often in your Friends' news feeds. Do this regularly!
- Shape your comments in the form of questions, rather than as straight statements, so as to encourage others to respond.
- End a post with a call to action to increase engagement. 'Click Like if you agree' or 'Please Share this' are two examples.
- From time to time, use Notes to post longer content.
- Don't post too many updates as people will either 'hide' them or even 'unlike' you if they feel they are being inundated. One to two posts per day at most, one to two posts per week at least.
- Post comments in response to comments and thumbs up. Even a 'Thank you' to a compliment is better than nothing!
- Do not automate and duplicate your updates across other media. For instance, you can send many more tweets per day than Facebook updates whilst still keeping people engaged.
- Share links to interesting content posted by others so that your feeds are not limited to your own school, thus increasing the level of general interest.
- A useful general guide is to only post on Facebook if you think it will encourage your followers to click 'like' or post a comment. Not only does this ensure that your posts are likely to be read but it also increases your visibility in others' news feeds.
- Consider making a schedule so that various administrators have complete control at certain times, such as before and after school. This keeps your content fresh.
- If someone gives you a sizeable donation, ensure that you favourite their page. Adding a comment to one of their posts or tagging them in a status update will earn even more brownie points!
- Ask some of your school community to give comments and thumbs

up to your status updates. Others seeing such engagement taking place are more likely to engage themselves. A rough rule of thumb is looking for one comment and five thumbs-ups for every thousand fans.
- Share links to your other social media sites.
- Post your updates when your followers are likely to log onto Facebook. They are more likely to appear in their news feeds as a result.
- Try the occasional post at the weekend to see responses – you might pick up more 'likes' from people not engaging during the week.
- Have more than one admin person so that you do not lose access if someone leaves. Ensure that they have changed their settings to ensure that when they post they are doing so personally, rather than in an admin capacity.

iii. Increasing your Facebook community
- Add a Facebook icon to your website's homepage and include one in every edition of your newsletter.
- Add a Facebook link in the email signature used by staff; encourage volunteers, parents and others to do likewise.
- Email your school community letting them know that you are on Facebook and asking them to like your page.
- Take every opportunity to tell people that you are on Facebook, including the school's suppliers.
- Try asking a question in all your communications that requires people to answer through your Facebook page.
- Make it a priority to gain 25 likes so that you can claim your vanity URL (i.e. a more personalised website address), which will make it easier for people to find you. (If you are already at 25 likes or over ensure that you have claimed it!)

iv. Things to try
- Events – Facebook has a number of useful features which makes it easier to run events. Go to www.events.fb.com for more information.
- Build a group so that you can target certain people in different ways to others, such as by pushing harder for donations or support. Go to www.groups.fb.com for more information.

Twitter

Twitter might not be as popular as Facebook but it still has hundreds of millions of users. It is a quick and easy way to alert potential donors of your funding needs.

i. Getting started
- You can sign up to Twitter here: twitter.com/signup?lang=engb
- Make sure that your username tallies with other social media platforms, including your website.

ii. General tips
- Ensure that your privacy settings are open, so that everyone can see your tweets. Similarly, add a location to your tweets, enabling people nearby to find you (although if you are administering the account as a volunteer from home then keep this unticked).
- Aim for a ratio of 1:1 between the number of followers you have and the number you are following. This shows that you are engaged in Twitter, while encouraging more people to follow and engage with you. So aim to follow those who choose to follow you. If you do find that you have to block certain followers, such as spammers, then follow large charities and educational establishments you admire to maintain the ratio.
- Regularly favourite tweets – it highlights important messages to your followers and creates goodwill which will often be reciprocated.
- Do not follow hundreds of people if you only have a handful of followers. You might be taken for a spammer and not be followed!
- If you have a lot of followers then consider segmenting them into lists, such as donors, volunteers etc. Do this by going to your Profile and Settings and creating a Twitter List.
- Use hashtags to organise your tweets and attract new followers but do not go overboard – one or two hashtags at most!
- When retweeting, always add a comment so that your avatar and name is highlighted rather than those belonging to the account behind the original tweet. If you want the original Twitterer to see your retweet then it is better to 'manually retweet': copy the original tweet into a new one, delete the name of the user you are retweeting and put 'RT' before, and a colon straight after, their username. Put your own message at the start so people can see why you have retweeted the message.

- Don't be afraid to repost tweets that have particular relevance or interest.

iii. Content
- Ask followers to sign up to your newsletter as well as to retweet important messages. However, keep such direct requests to a minimum – no more than 10% of your tweets.
- Keep your tweets topical and timely. For instance 'New e-newsletter going out tomorrow – sign up here!'
- Pictures, videos, quotes and statistics all make powerful content.
- Use the free service bit.ly (www.bitly.com) to shrink long web links, giving you more space for your main message, as well as to provide analysis on engagement levels.
- Engage with other Twitterers – if you just tweet your own content and news, you will not engage nearly as many people as you would by retweeting and replying to other's tweets.
- Don't ask for donations directly on Twitter – it is not the right medium. Instead ask people to subscribe to your newsletter or go to your website where they might give instead.
- Explore third-party Twitter apps to make your tweets stand out. Twitdom provides an easily searchable directory of over 2,000 different apps (www.twitdom.com).
- Consider running the occasional survey over Twitter to gain feedback and engage followers. Twtpoll has a small cost but is perhaps the best known. (www.twtpoll.com).

iv. Timings
- 4 to 6 tweets spaced out over the course of the day.
- Don't send all your tweets at one time. Most tweets will become obsolete and go unread 90 minutes after they have been sent so people not following Twitter at the time you tweet will miss everything.
- Consider using a social media management tool, such as HootSuite, to space your tweets to go throughout the day.
- Don't send too many tweets (unless you are particularly engaging!). Ten is the maximum for most users before followers start zoning out and skipping such messages.

Stand-out features
There are approximately 25,000 schools in England and Wales. More of

them are fundraising and most want the same kind of things. It is therefore essential that you make your fundraising requests stand out, particularly if you are going to big foundations.

i. What do funders look for?
Imagine that you are a funder and you are giving away books for school libraries. You have 25 'libraries' to give away. What would you look for in an application?

Let's say 1% of schools apply. That's 250 schools. You can be pretty certain that each one will say that they are short of books and that their children would do better with more. There will also be plenty of information given about the different schools, no doubt with standard facts such as the type of school and the particular geographical location.

Now imagine that you have to read each of these applications. That's 250 well-deserving schools all saying the same thing. How would you feel as you worked your way through them? You would certainly be bored, you would almost certainly start skimming applications and you would probably slip quite a few unread ones into the rejection pile.

ii. Finding the stand-out feature
So to avoid having your application ignored and discarded, you need to make your projects have at least one stand-out feature. How you do this is part of the art of fundraising and there is no simple formula to follow. However, consider whether anyone else is likely to be submitting something similar to yours. For instance, returning to the school library example, you might approach a well-known author asking them to open your new library if successful. Or you might have a quote from a well-known figure saying why your library is so needed. These will stand out from the normal 'Our children really need this' refrain.

All the big charities regularly bring together various people to brainstorm unique points for bids and it is worth you doing the same. Give a little brief on what your prospect funder is interested in and then ask participants to come up with something unique and original. Invariably, someone will come up with something workable and if you have more than one item all the better. Here are some good fillers to get you going:

- Include quotes by your children saying why they think funding is important
- Hand-write, rather than type, the covering letter

- Include pictures by your children showing what a post-funding image of the school or project would look like
- Have someone who is already supporting you make the request on your behalf, explaining why they give to you (even better if they say their support is dependent on a successful outcome)
- Personalise your cover envelope, from simple stand-out colours to 'Please help' tags written by your children
- Enclose a sweet with a note saying 'Thought you might like this while you worked through the application'.

iii. Make sure your point is noted

Once you have identified your unique feature, you need to convey it quickly. If you are application 177 out of 200 and the first 176 are all saying the same thing then the grant manager is unlikely to read the whole of your proposal unless given reason. If your stand-out point is tucked away on Page 4 then it might never be read! So put your unique points up front, in the first two or three lines of your application or proposal. That's not to say that you do not put in the standard arguments, such as a library will help with your children's reading. It's just that you put them in further down.

One final word on deprived areas: if your school is in a deprived area then do of course mention it. However, you should still go and find another unique feature. There are thousands of schools that can say they are in deprived areas and if you use this argument alone then there is a good chance that you will miss out to a more interesting application that includes other items. The same goes for 'outstanding' schools.

Storytelling

It is universally agreed that the best fundraisers use stories to secure donations. Why? Because telling stories brings funding requests to life and most decisions to give are made with the heart rather than the head.

i. Stories to hand

To be a successful story teller, you should have one or two stories that you can readily narrate. Each should ultimately encourage a listener to give to one of the projects for which you are fundraising.

For instance, if you are looking for laptop computers, you could say:

'We are looking for laptops for Y6. This will improve their maths results and help them when they join secondary school'.

Alternatively, you could say:

'Tommy was struggling with maths. He hated the subject and was always near the bottom of the class. He'd had extra attention from the teacher and the school paid for extra support outside normal hours – all to no avail. We then gave him a laptop, with a maths programme loaded onto it. The results were amazing. Tommy's performance shot up and he showed real enthusiasm for the subject. He's now in the top group of boys and is even talking about becoming a mathematician. Of course, it also means that his teacher can spend more time teaching the rest of the class rather than Tommy alone. It's a win-win all round. In fact, we've decided to buy laptops for every child in Year 6. We simply need to find the £8,000 needed to fund it – the secondary schools won't know what's hit them!'

This second, personalised approach will certainly raise you more support as it brings the need and project to life.

ii. Why stories work
Scientifically speaking, a story locks into both the analytical and the emotional parts of the brain. If you only have one of these elements then the full impact is lost. Similarly, by introducing a real character you bring the need and effects of the project across much more effectively. People can empathise with characters, and clearly enjoy doing so, as witnessed by the amount of fiction we read. However, unlike a novel, whose ending is predetermined, you are allowing a potential donor to alter the outcome of your story. That is something that many of us are unable to do in our everyday lives and is one reason why so many donors say that giving can be such fun.

iii. Anonymity and embellishments
Clearly, if there is any chance of your main character being stigmatised then change the name or make them unidentifiable. And, of course, you should not fabricate your stories – if none of the benefits are true then you will be found out and will never see a donation again from the donor. However, most good stories have a degree of embellishment to bring them to life, so make them as colourful and lively as you can.

Networking
Part of being successful at raising funds is the ability to network. Although

to some, networking conjures up images of 'pushy' and 'fake' individuals, good networking involves providing mutually-beneficial interactions that help all parties concerned. And the more you network the more likely you are to find that individual who has been looking for a school like yours to support.

i. Pre-networking activities

- Write down what you would like to achieve from the outset. For example: 'Speak to 5 people'; 'Find a volunteer'; 'Set up a meeting with a potential donor'.
- Keep your goals manageable and relatively simple. For instance, 'Arranging a coffee and chat with a potential supporter' is much more likely to be achieved than 'Securing a donation'. People rarely have the time or the inclination to go into any great depth when talking at events or receptions so simply ask for a follow-up chat if there seems to be some mutual interest.

ii. Points to consider while networking

- Remove the pressure that networking can invoke. For instance, if you think that you need to secure a large donation while meeting and mixing with people, you will be considerably stressed and most likely very disappointed. Rather, change your mindset so that you see networking as a means to not only further your needs, but also to provide help and assistance to others.
- Try not to monopolise the conversation – in general, less talking is better!
- Try to find out as much as possible about the person you're talking to, particularly what interests them. They will only support you if their interests tie in with what your school is doing.
- Approach single people and groups of three, rather than pairs or larger groups – they are much easier to join and start a conversation.
- Watch body language – a couple or group of three facing out towards the room is usually a good guide that they are open to having someone else join them; conversely, closed groups generally do not welcome newcomers.
- If you take a business card from someone, consider writing something on the back unique to that person which will help you remember them.
- Move round the room, not spending too long with any one person

(however tempting!) A simple means of moving on is to say 'It's been very good to talk to you. Now I must talk to X. Is there anybody I can introduce you to or send your way if I bump into them?'

iii. Post-event or activity
- Act quickly on any leads. If you leave it too late, initial enthusiasm will be lost.
- Review your efforts. Did you speak to everyone you wanted to? Are you speaking to more people over time? Are you speaking to the right people? The key is to keep learning and developing!

Psychology of influence

The principles of influence and persuasion are invaluable when fundraising, just as they are in other fields. The classic book on the subject is *Influence* by Robert B Cialdini. It is widely used by professional fundraisers and has been a recommended text within the big fundraising charities for many years.

To apply this to your own situation, use the following six principles.

1. Authority
This principle is perhaps more readily apparent in a school environment than anywhere else. After all, 'See the Head Teacher' strikes more fear into most children than 'See the Drama Teacher'! In other words, the opinions and actions of those perceived as having greater authority carry more weight than those with less.

So, in terms of fundraising, where time is limited, the head teacher might only become involved in 5-figure donations and above, the deputy head or chair of governors with 4-figure ones and heads of year or subject specialists in smaller gifts still. This should not be set in stone though. For instance, the head teacher might meet a prospective 4-figure donor where an impasse seems to have been reached – that extra authority might just sway the donor to give.

2. Liking
People are more easily persuaded by those they like than those they don't. We often share the same values with people we like and are keen to show willing as a result. Conversely, it is tempting to be unhelpful and uncooperative with those we do not like.

When dealing with donors, you can take this principle into account by ensuring that donors are chaperoned by like-minded individuals. For instance, when asking parents for a contribution you might ask a fellow parent to make the request – they will enthuse about the school and its impact on the children. Conversely, a hard-nosed businessman might be better served by the bursar or business manager, who could mutually agree the need to keep a tight rein on the budget (something that probably wouldn't go down too well with the parents!).

3. Reciprocity

This is the mechanism that makes people feel that they need to return a favour when one is done to them. It is this principle which guides certain charities to give away free pens and other items in direct mail campaigns.

Using this knowledge, you might wish to offer lunch to a big donor, give special tours of the school or have your children outline your needs. All these things take a degree of effort, which in turn implicitly call for something back in return. Obviously, don't abuse this principle – creating too much 'guilt' is likely to backfire in the end.

4. Scarcity

People value things that are scarce – they want them more than the mundane or commonplace. Books signed by their authors and limited edition cars are classic examples of using this technique to increase desire and, ultimately, sales.

You can create this sense of scarcity in your fundraising by developing unique projects and by offering exclusive benefits. With the former, you might approach a donor to talk about the cutting-edge science laboratory you are looking to build or the exceptional circumstances your pupils face. With the latter, you might talk about naming rights for a new building or classroom, with only one donor's name available to be 'put in lights'. In each case, your argument for giving is strengthened by the scarcity principle.

5. Consistency

People like to feel that they are consistent with their values and commitments. The challenge in fundraising is to find out what those values are in prospective donors and appeal to them.

You might affirm a value you have spotted in one of your donors by saying, 'A gift by you of £10,000 to buy these musical instruments will help fulfil your wish of seeing every young person have the opportunity to play.' You can also use this principle to bring about change when people are not being consistent. For instance, it can be difficult to get pledges fulfilled after an event, where initial enthusiasm wanes the day after. Pointing out why the pledge was given in the first place can be an effective spur to action for the person making the pledge.

6. Social proof

People are wary of the unknown and of looking foolish. They are much more likely to be persuaded if you can point to similar situations and scenarios where someone has taken the path you are proposing.

In practice, someone might be giving you £200 a year but have the capacity to give much more. You might let this donor know that ten donors give £500 a year and two give £1,500. Without this knowledge, the donor might think his £200 is the largest amount given and is excessively generous. Similarly, when you need to raise much more money than you have ever done before, you might appeal to circumstances in a school or organisation that has attempted similar activities. For example, 'A local firm paid £60,000 over three years for naming rights of X's new swimming pool and we are looking for a similar amount'.

These simple principles are invaluable in unlocking funds, whatever the size of the prospective donor. So try to ensure that any person who fundraises for you is aware of the principles and has the necessary information to follow through. In that way, everybody knows such things as the size of the largest donation and maximises the overall impact of your fundraising effort.

10. Fundraising tools to give you an edge

Chapter 10 in a nutshell

In Chapter 10, a range of techniques for adding value to a fundraising drive is described. Each technique will enable the fundraiser to increase supporters' level of engagement with the cause, yielding higher financial and motivational returns.

11
DEALING WITH REJECTIONS

If you have not been rejected by a prospect then you are not trying hard enough! Unfortunately, there is no getting around this fact. However, rejections are far from being the end of the world and can indeed be helpful.

i. Protecting yourself psychologically

For some fundraisers (usually the better ones but not always!), being rejected causes little concern. The reason for this is how they view the rejection. Follow their lead by adopting the following attitudes:

- Depersonalise the rejection – unless you are deliberately rude and offensive (or look particularly untrustworthy!) it is very unlikely that a proposal has been rejected because of you personally.
- Sometimes there is no real reason – if a funder has no more money or they are not considering applications for another year there is not much you can do, however brilliant your proposition.
- Consider it a learning opportunity – use rejections as occasions to improve your fundraising. If you can take one element of learning from every rejection, you will soon turn into a brilliant fundraiser!

ii. Responding to funders who reject you

While it may be tempting simply to write the funder off, particularly if you have put a lot of work into a request, you will be well-advised to build up your network and not burn bridges. Try putting the following four questions to the person rejecting you to turn a negative into a positive.

Can the proposition be improved?

You should ask if there was anything in the proposition that could be changed or improved.

Few people willingly wish to cause upset so, unless it comes across clearly that you will not be offended by any criticism given, you will not gain any meaningful feedback. You can build such a feeling of openness by asking follow-up questions when the first tentative comments on your proposition are given. A quick, hypothetical conversation will give you the idea:

Fundraiser: *I would be most interested to hear if there was any way you think I could improve the proposition?*

Funder: *Well, perhaps it could do with a bit more impact, but not really, it was very good.*

Fundraiser: *Yes, I was a little uncertain about how impactful it was. Can you say a little more?*

Can we try again?
Just because someone says 'no' to you, it doesn't mean that it will always be a 'no'. Children instinctively know this, though I would suggest that if you want to be successful in your fundraising over the long-term then it is better to find the win-win scenarios rather than breaking down funders by exhaustion!

The best way to find out whether you can reapply is to ask directly. A simple 'Is it worth reapplying?' followed by a 'When would be the best time to do this?' is all that is needed. Often you will find that the funder is very clear on what needs to change if reapplying or will suggest an alternative type of project to put forward. However, if the response is very hesitant and unconvincing, cut your losses and move on.

Do you know of anyone else who might fund this?
A lot of people do not like to give rejections so are very open to exchanges where a balance of power is restored. So by offering them the opportunity to give you a lead you are also offering them the chance to wipe out any sense that they might have been mean or unkind to you (i.e. to remove any 'cognitive dissonance' they have in relation to their normally kind and helpful selves).

Would you like to receive our newsletter?
Unless the person rejecting you is never likely to support you, it would be a big advantage if you could maintain a relationship with them. Even if it is a yearly update you will remain in their consciousness and you will be slightly ahead of those who make contact out of the blue.

Chapter 11 in a nutshell

Rejection is a simple fact of life in all fundraising situations. This chapter advises the fundraiser how to deal with rejection and, ideally, how to turn it to advantage.

12
OVERCOMING DONOR APATHY AND STALLING

Restarting stalled funding requests

Funding requests which have been stuck with a funder for a good amount of time are a common but difficult stage to navigate. It is very easy to do nothing and hope for the best. After all, if you contact someone to see whether they will give, the law of percentages says that you are likely to be rejected. Nobody likes being rebuffed and even professional fundraisers struggle with this stage – I have spent many a time chivvying fundraisers to follow up on their initial approaches!

i. Why bother chasing?

The sad fact is that many people and organisations never get round to giving unless properly nudged. So the interesting proposal that temporarily gets put to one side by a local business gathers more dust when no one reminds the owner that they were going to action it. Or the foundation that has two very strong proposals but only one funding opportunity at the next trustees' meeting waits to see which school will ring and show that it really wants the cash.

ii. Giving yourself confidence

As human beings, we protect ourselves, avoiding imaginary rejections and worst-case scenarios. 'I was shocked by how much you were asking for!', 'Are you for real?' or 'Give me the name of the head teacher so I can have you fired!' are some inner-voices that you may hear before following up.

Remember, though, that if you have made your approach after having given some thought as to the donor's motivation then it is very unlikely that anyone will take offence, even if the proposition does not hit the mark. In fact, you are more likely to receive an apology if the answer is 'no'. Again, this is simply human nature. For instance, if you went to someone's house and they specially offered you your favourite drink, say red wine, but you preferred white for a change, then it would be extraordinary if you took offence. Instead, you would most likely be apologetic that such effort was being spurned and you might revert back to the favoured tipple to lessen your unease; it is the same with fundraising.

So before you follow up, tell yourself why you thought that the proposition would be beneficial to the donor. Once you are clear, undertake the follow-up.

You might also like to try some of the physical techniques that some people swear by. Here are a few:

- Stretch and beat your chest (best tried alone!)
- Take some deep, slow breaths
- Sing some scales (apparently this is good for adding resonance to your voice, which at the very least will make you sound more confident).

iii. Overcoming stalling or lethargy

The chances are that on following up you will get a response along the lines of 'We have not had time to look at your proposal yet' or 'It's very interesting but we need more time to consider'. You need tactics to overcome these delays and facilitate decisions.

There are two considerations to take into account: time factors and donor motivations.

Time factors

The idea here is to create a sense of urgency in the prospect's mind. The way to do this is to give a deadline, however contrived. For instance, would the examples below spur you into action more than a typical, but anodyne, 'When you have time, please do consider our proposal':

- If we do not gain the funding by the end of the month, we will not be able to put on our school play.
- Children are at risk while we have this old equipment in place.
- The local MP is visiting the school next month and I would love to be able to say that you are our biggest donor when she arrives.

Donor motivations

As described on pages 31-34, these are an essential consideration when trying to encourage someone to take a decision or to pay attention to what you are saying. For example, if you know the donor is interested by the *social* motivation and there is an opportunity to open the school fete then let the prospect know! Here are some other examples:

Philanthropic
- If we don't help these children soon they will be at risk to criminal gangs or extremism.

Affinity
- If we don't raise the money soon then those in your child's year will never have access to the new facilities.

Mutual benefit
- If you commit in the next few days then we can mention your sponsorship in the upcoming newsletter going to 500 parents.

Social
- The head teacher and chair of governors are free for lunch next week and I am hoping that we can finalise your donation so that you can join them.

iv. Brainstorms

Talking to others when you get stuck with a donor can be very helpful. A different perspective can often be all that is needed to unlock the funder.

If you have several fundraisers then you can make such a meeting a regular one. Each fundraiser can then bring one or two prospects where they want help and ideas as to how to move forward.

When running such a meeting, ensure that the briefings are short. Nobody needs to hear every last detail about the prospect. Instead, explain:

- The history of the funder in relation to the school, including past gifts
- What is being asked for
- What the donor's giving motivation is thought to be
- Where the block is occurring
- What has been tried so far but has not worked.

If you are running through several prospects then limit the amount of time you allocate to each, such as 10 minutes, otherwise you risk wasting time in unproductive discussion.

v. Knowing when to give up

Sometimes being a good fundraiser is simply knowing when to stop. You will inevitably come across donors who will string you along for months and even years if you let them. This can happen for a variety of reasons, including the enjoyment of being chased and the hope that donor benefits will be given even when a donation is not forthcoming.

This is a difficult call to make, particularly when you are being offered untold riches. However, factors that imply that you should cut your losses include:

- Excuses for not giving start to repeat. That is, you have heard the same excuse before, despite answering it
- The donor is taking much, much longer than other donors in a similar position
- The donor is much less forthcoming when talking with other staff or volunteers
- The donation will be transformational but there is always one stumbling block in the way.

Once you think that your cultivation of a donor is not going to result in a donation however hard you try, then be firm with yourself. You need to stop the telephone calls and any other solicitation techniques that you have been using. By all means, keep the donor on the newsletter list but stop the invitations to school events or any other benefits you might have been giving – you are not giving away free lunches!

One final point on this area is in relation to other staff or volunteers wanting to keep the donor approaches going. For instance, if the head teacher insists that she wants to see a donor at the next event, you would be foolish to completely disregard this. However, I would try and raise your concerns. A light-hearted approach is often best, such as 'Two to one that we are wasting our time with that one!'

Engaging non-participants

If you sent out a fundraiser to all parents and got a 25% response rate you might be impressed. But what about the other 75%? The fact is that most schools have a much higher rate of non-participants than participants. Given how many households your school serves, those non-responders are likely to amount to a considerable lost opportunity.

i. Why we don't focus on non-responders

There are a number of factors why most schools do not expend time and effort in this area. A typical reason is not being sure that the effort is worth it. This particularly happens when the focus is on the immediate. For example, you need computer tablets right now and it seems a needless distraction to spend time looking to engage those who might not immediately give anything worthwhile. However, if you can focus on the lifetime value of your donors, or what they will give over the whole period of their relationship with you, then you start to realise that a little effort now can bring substantial rewards.

Another reason we do not expend effort on finding out such information is that we do not want to open ourselves to the possibility of hearing anything negative. Yet, the most likely reason that these people do not become involved is because they do not think anyone will notice. Typical responses will be 'I didn't know anything about it', 'I didn't know how to give', or 'I didn't think it was important'.

Certain schools are also worried about putting undue pressure on those with little capacity to give. However, by having a number of non-financial options to support you can involve these people. For instance, rallying other parents or collecting second-hand clothes to sell and recycle are fairly widespread non-financial activities a good many schools take part in. Whatever you decide would help you, by stressing that it is not only money that is of interest, then you remove limited finances as an option to opt-out.

ii. Problem solving

Once you have identified the issues you can start overcoming them. Come up with a solution for each problem identified and allocate someone to tackle it in a given timeframe. Most issues should be fairly straightforward, with the most common covered below:

Not knowing how to support
You should really have a web page or set of pages which show all the ways that you can receive support. At the least, have one page on your website dedicated to this.

Not of interest
If the ways to support your school are all of the same type then you will exclude a good many potential supporters. For instance, if your school only offers cake bakes and coffee mornings then it will exclude a good many people who have little interest in this.

Apathy
General apathy is likely to be a key reason for non-involvement and can be a difficult problem to tackle. One way to overcome this is to try and

'normalise' the idea of involvement. For instance, where you have an activity in which the majority of your external community is involved you can encourage non-participants into taking part simply by pointing out that by not participating they are the exception.

You can also overcome apathy by highlighting or praising donors and helpers. A simple list of every parent who supported or gave time in the last term with an accompanying expression of thanks is a good way to express gratitude as well as to spur non-participants into action.

iii. Regularly reviewing

Unfortunately, it is a fact of life that however dynamic and pro-active you are with your engagement activities, some people will disengage or simply not take part. While it is easy to give up on this group – and there will be a certain hard-core group you can never motivate – regularly give thought as to how you might engage non-supporters. A once-a-term brainstorm is a good way of doing this.

12. Overcoming donor apathy and stalling

Chapter 12 in a nutshell

Even without an outright rejection (as in Chapter 11), there are times when fundraising approaches receive slow, uncertain or disappointing responses. This chapter outlines those situations where the fundraiser can take useful remedial action – and those where it can be best simply to draw a line and move on.

13
SOMEONE HAS GIVEN!

Good news if you've reached this stage! Of course, you will be more elated by a £20,000 donation from a foundation than a £20 donation from a parent. However, the latter might have been more of a sacrifice than the former, so have a policy for accepting all donations, irrespective of size.

Recognition tables

Size is important and how you accept large and small donations will differ accordingly. The standard approach is to create a recognition table, stating what every donor receives in return for a certain size of gift. For example:

Gift size	Thank you response
£0-£100	Standard thank you from head teacher
£101-999	Personally signed letter from head teacher
£1,000-£4,999	Personally signed letter from head teacher, plus invitation for personalised tour of school
£4,999-£19,999	Personally signed letter from head teacher, plus invitation for personalised tour of school, plus lunch
£20,000+	Opportunity to have a classroom or building named after somebody

Table 6 Recognition table

When creating such a table, try and do so before you actually start receiving donations. Not only will it help you bring in gifts but it also avoids problems such as donors being offered inappropriate rewards because nobody is fully aware of what should be given.

Recognition and donor motivations

As always, donor motivations are essential when dealing with funders. So when you come to thank someone bear in mind what caused them to give; where a large gift warrants special thanks, the donor motivation should inform its expression. Here are some examples:

- Being guest of honour at a school event (*philanthropic* motivation)
- Being given a personal tour of the building by the head teacher (*affinity* motivation)
- Lunch with the head teacher, governors and the local MP (*social* motivation)
- Naming rights to a building (*mutual benefit* motivation).

Shrinking violets

Not all donors want recognition. Indeed some will positively shy away from recognition - those of the *philanthropic* persuasion can often fall into this category, particularly where there is a fear of being inundated with funding requests as a result of publicity.

With this in mind, always check that public recognition is wanted. Note as well that there is a difference between a donor being self-deprecating and someone generally not wanting publicity – the latter is usually fairly obvious, not least because it is normally stated in very clear terms!

It's too good to be true!

It is worth undertaking financial and character checks when receiving unsolicited, large donations. For instance, it is not unknown for some companies facing potential bankruptcy to make large pledges to charitable organisations in the hope that any favourable publicity will lead to an uptake in business which will subsequently fund the donation. Consequently, take bank and personal references from large, unknown benefactors. Any legitimate donor is unlikely to raise an objection, whereas an unscrupulous one might well!

Chapter 13 in a nutshell

Although the receipt of a donation may appear to be the end of the fundraising journey, it should in fact be the starting point for two new phases of activity.

This chapter looks at the first of these phases – ensuring that the donation is fully and carefully recognised, and that mistakes in accepting inappropriate gifts are guarded against.

Chapter 14 will consider the following phase, of ongoing donor development.

14
KEEPING DONORS HAPPY

If a prospect only ever hears from you when you want money then you have a problem! To avoid this, fundraising departments have taken to developing stewardship programmes. These engage donors between gifts so that when the right time comes to make another funding request, it falls on receptive ears.

Who goes into the stewardship programme?

The short answer to this question is: anyone who might give you a donation.

Whenever you make contact with a new prospect then you should check whether they would be happy to hear from you again. Assuming the answer is in the affirmative, they can be entered into your stewardship programme.

Databases

Whether you use a dedicated fundraising database or simply an Excel spreadsheet, it is important that you keep a list of everyone in your stewardship programme. Items you should record as an absolute minimum are:

- Name
- Address
- Contact details
- History of giving
- Dates of contact, including the name of the communication or engagement activity.

The last date of engagement is important – if it is longer than 3 months then your prospect will likely be losing interest or at the very least be feeling unappreciated.

Ideally, you should also be recording other details (see Segmentation, page 128). However, it is a delicate balancing act between noting too much and too little. If in doubt, err on the side of too much.

Finally, remember that you need to comply with Data Protection laws (ico.org.uk/for-organisations/guide-to-data-protection).

Activities to keep your donors engaged

Regularly communicating with donors and prospects is important to build trust and maximise your support. Sending a mixture of communications throughout the year, rather than contacting donors simply when you want or need a donation, is likely to lead to more donations. To do this, you should create a plan of engagement activities to run throughout the school year, being a mixture of:

1. News items
2. Thank-you notes
3. Invitations
4. Funding requests

It is important to note that the last item, funding requests, should be used sparingly, every two or three communications at most. You are then treating your donors and prospects more as partners and supporters, rather than as cash cows – the latter being deeply off-putting!

In terms of how you might fulfil these stewardship activities, consider using the following as opportunities to engage with your funders and prospects:

1. A thank you every time a campaign finishes or a milestone is reached (this could be in person, by phone or by text depending on the importance of the donor)
2. Invitations to school events and activities, such as sports or prize-giving days
3. In-person meetings, with the head teacher if warranted
4. End of year reports (see End of year reports on page 128 for more details)
5. Updates or invites to project openings
6. Communications highlighting student achievements
7. General news updates, such as notable successes or indeed failures that need outside support.

In addition, try and include individual messages from the most senior members of your school, such as the head teacher and the chair of governors – there is nothing more dispiriting for a major donor than to find an exciting and inspiring fundraising campaign has no real interest from the head!

In terms of frequency, you should be contacting everybody in your stewardship programme every month and certainly not leaving it longer than three months. Whether that is a newsletter, email, tweet, text, event, phone call or lunch does not matter too much – just keep your school firmly fixed in their minds.

Segmentation (personalisation)

Depending on the amount of time and resource available, you might consider segmenting those in your stewardship programme. For instance, if you notice that someone always gives to a music appeal but never to one for sport then it will likely be useful to note that down. By personalising subsequent communications and approaches, you will make the donor feel more appreciated and listened to which, in turn, should lead to more donations.

Types of segmentation which you might wish to try include:

- By amount
- By subject
- By type of donor, for instance parents or alumni.

End of year reports

The end of the school year provides a good opportunity to thank all your donors over past three terms and prepare the ground for September.

Follow these points to create a feelgood communication which will inspire your donors:

1. List all the projects for which you raised funds over the year and explain how support has made a difference. Use photos and quotes from children.

2. Give an overview of the school, ideally painting a picture of an organisation moving forward. Include achievements, developments, changes in staff etc.

3. Showcase at least one of your biggest funders. This raises expectations and aspirations in others, encouraging them to give more. Highlight any benefits your donors received as again this might encourage future donations from those desiring similar advantages.

4. Use this communication as an information communication, avoiding any temptation to ask for support. The possible exception to this is

parents and others linked to the year group leaving your school – if there is a feeling of happy times and gratitude then support might be forthcoming.

5. Use a mixture of visual and statistical information – different people respond to different presentational styles.

6. Personalise the communication, such as by using first names and stating how much support someone gave during the year. If you do not have such information then take the opportunity to start gathering such data. You might wish to go to extra lengths for your biggest supporters, such as an end of year lunch with the head teacher.

7. Keep contact details of those leaving your school. They are potential supporters and keeping them warm and onside is not difficult. Even a once a year communication giving a school update will keep them connected.

8. Provide contact details and an opportunity for comments or feedback You might pick up useful information and it shows that you are receptive to donors' needs.

Being contactable

Whenever you communicate with your donors and prospects, provide a means for feedback and suggestions. If you have begun to build a reputation for being receptive to new ideas and opportunities then you will be surprised at how many people are willing to help and open doors for you. And there is nothing nicer than receiving an unforeseen donation from someone completely unexpected!

Expanding your workforce

It is extremely easy to neglect stewardship – most people much prefer to undertake the activities which lead directly to donations – while stewardship programmes are often the first to go when manpower is limited. Yet it is vitally important to undertake this relationship-building work!

One way to ensure that you do not neglect this area, particularly if resources or time are tight, is to involve pupils in certain aspects. They will learn invaluable skills such as dealing with different people and running projects on time and in budget. In addition, many donors would rather hear from the ultimate beneficiaries, the children. You might also find that you have parents with marketing, publishing or other related backgrounds. Make use of them!

Whether it is children or adults covering the tasks, ensure that you have them all covered. You might not see the results immediately but this area leads to many of the largest donations.

Chapter 14 in a nutshell

This chapter underlines the importance of cultivating prospects and donors over the long term to establish strong and enduring relationships. The essentials of a stewardship programme are outlined, including the need to accurately record donor and prospect details, and to keep individuals engaged and informed in ways appropriate to their particular interests.

15
CAMPAIGNS – BRINGING IT ALL TOGETHER

So far we have looked at the key points to consider when you are fundraising for a project. However, as your fundraising becomes more advanced and developed, you should consider running Campaigns. These bring additional structure to your fundraising and firmly establish the discipline in the minds of your school community.

There are three types of Campaign: Annual, Capital and Endowment. The Annual Campaign is the first type you should tackle. Once you have had some success with that, ideally at least two or three years' worth, then you can consider adding a Capital or Endowment Campaign. I say 'either' because both these campaigns ask funders to make larger gifts than normal and detract from your Annual Campaign – if you run both at the same time, you will likely fail in all areas unless your fundraising is very developed and you have numerous contacts.

Annual Campaigns
i. Purpose
The annual campaign has two main aims:

> **Provide funds for operational purposes**
> For instance, you might have ambitious plans to upgrade your sporting facilities. As a result, you might theme all your fundraising for the year around 'sport'.

> **Provide a free flow of new major donors**
> If your largest donor gives you £1,000 a year then running a capital campaign for a new building is likely to fall flat, despite the need. Indeed, when it comes to capital campaigns you really want to have at least 40% of the target raised before going public. So you need to have a good number of big donors already committed to your school. The Annual Campaign is the way to draw them in.

ii. Content
Three elements make up your Annual Campaign:
1. Case statement
2. Marketing Plan
3. Implementation and Monitoring.

15. Campaigns – bringing it all together

We will discuss these in turn.

Case Statement

The Case Statement is largely taken from the Case for Support (see page 88) and should show:

- What type of school you are, for example 'A secondary school in a rural area'
- What the campaign is about. For example, 'Literacy'
- How much funding is being sought
- What the needs are that are being met through the campaign. For example, 'Improved GCSE pass-rates for English'
- The benefits to donors in participating. For instance, 'Improved employability prospects of the pupils'
- Details of how support can be given.

In terms of writing this up, I would use the structure detailed in Trust and statutory applications on page 56. What you will end up with is a document that can be handed to existing and potential donors, volunteers, staff and anybody else who might become involved. While you will no doubt wish to tailor any proposals to big donors, all the key information for those kind of personalised proposals can be taken from this document.

Marketing plan

Once you have your Case Statement, you can work out how you are going to put it to potential donors.

- **Gift Tables**

  Clear segmentation and targeting of your prospects is key to your success. Unfortunately, many fundraisers do not do this well. For instance, it is quite common to see schools aiming to raise, for example, £10,000 by targeting 500 donors at £20 each. This very rarely works in practice.

  Much more common in real life is one donor giving between 20% and 50% of the target, with a few others giving slightly less than the main sponsor. These are the key prospects and need careful work and handling. Conversely, the final 10% might come from all the small donors.

In order that this phenomenon is reflected, fundraisers use 'gift tables' to segment and weight the importance of their prospects before a campaign. The table below shows an example gift table for a £50,000 project.

Gift Range	Donors Needed	Prospects needed (ratio)	Ratio of prospects to donors	Total
£10,000	1	7	7:1	£10,000
£5,000		12	6:1	£10,000
£2,500		16	4:1	£10,000
£1,000	10	30	3:1	£10,000
£250	20	50	2.5:1	£5,000
£100	25	50	2:1	£2,500
<£100	50	100	2:1	£2,500

Table 7 A Gift Table for a £50,000 Campaign

This is very different from the '500 people-each-giving-a uniform-£100' approach. Instead:

- 265 prospects will be approached with the hope of gaining 112 donations.
- 7 donors will give over 50% of the target; 75 donors will give 5%.
- The 'failure' rate amongst prospects falls in line with the amount being requested. So, for instance, in the table above you would expect to approach seven prospects capable of giving £10,000 before gaining your top gift, but would only need to approach two lower level targets for every gift under £100.

- **Targeting**
    It should be clear from the gift table above that the majority of the fundraising effort should be aimed at the seven or so donors who are likely to give you 70% of your target. In other words, it is vital to segment your prospects so that they are approached in different ways. For instance, you may wish to target high-worth prospects with meetings and school visits. For lower-level ones, a letter might suffice. Look over Chapter 6 again to work through this area methodically.

15. Campaigns – bringing it all together

- **Leverage**

  If you can secure one of the larger amounts early in your campaign, it is sometimes possible to leverage the donation (with the sponsor's permission, of course!) For instance, you might send a mailing to the smaller prospects stating that Funder X is willing to match-fund any £1 given, up to a maximum of £10,000. This type of leverage is very attractive to potential donors and certainly worth setting up if you can – you might well achieve all your small donations through one simple request this way. For details see Match-giving on page 94.

- **Calendar of activities**

  To make your campaign highly effective, having a calendar of solicitation activities is very helpful. For instance, you may decide that in September you will launch the campaign to all prospects with a mailer, and then spend October meeting your high-level prospects, before sending another letter in November. Conversely, if you tried to fit things in haphazardly as time permitted, at best you would miss opportunities and at worst your campaign would lose all focus. See Bringing everything together on page 41 for more information on this area. The key element is that you have your main activities worked out before you start the campaign.

- **Gift Aid**

  Make sure that donations you receive can be gift-aided so that you do not miss out on the Government's top-up. If you are unable to register or find it too much trouble then use School Funding Network's service (www.schoolsfundingnetwork.co.uk) they can support any charitable campaign.

- **Gift acceptance policy**

  It is also worth having a gift acceptance policy so that supporters are thanked uniformly for their donations. A very simple example would be as follows:

  - Less than £1000 – Thank you letter from head teacher
  - £1001 - £10,000 – Tour of the school
  - £10,001+ - Lunch with head teacher/tour of the school.

See Recognition tables on page 123 for more information on this area.

15. Campaigns – bringing it all together

Implementation and Monitoring

Once you have your plan for the year in place, then it needs delivering. There are a few additional elements that need to be added for campaigns to the fundraising points raised earlier in the book. We will run through them below.

- **Campaign Director**

    You must have someone with the authority and time to oversee the campaign. Their job will be to:

    - Ensure that activities are carried out on time
    - Liaise with key stakeholders, such as the head teacher
    - Find resolutions to problems
    - Hold ultimate responsibility for the success of the campaign.

- **Testing ideas and approaches**

    As your annual campaign begins to become an integral part of your fundraising, you will want to test various factors as to their effectiveness in raising funds. For instance, length of letter or number of asks in a year are both items you may wish to test.
    Table 4 shows an example of two mailings being tested for effectiveness. From this you can see that while you may be reluctant to undertake the second mailing because of the initial cost, the figures clearly show it is the more profitable option to take in future.

	Mailing 1	Mailing 2
Number of prospects	100	100
Cost of mailing	£35	£200
Number of donors giving	15	20
Average gift	£20	£50
Total Revenue	£300	£1000
Net Income	£265	£800

Table 8 Testing the effectiveness of two mailings

- **Long term trends**

    One of the advantages of running an annual campaign is that you can monitor annual trends. This enables you to check that your efforts are becoming more effective over time. The following three tables show items that when measured will help inform an improvement in your school's fundraising over time.

15. Campaigns – bringing it all together

Year	Gross Income	Costs	Net income	Return on Investment
1	£8,100	£120	£7,980	6,650%
2	£14,931	£250	£14,681	5,972%
3	£34,320	£6,000	£28,320	572%
4	£89,175	£24,000	£76,975	372%
5	£147,445	£30,000	£129,045	491%

Table 9 Annual Campaign Effectiveness: Income

By plotting Costs and Net Income, and not just Gross Income, you gain a much clearer idea of what is and is not productive. For instance, this school has started investing more heavily in fundraising from Year 3. This might be due to the employment of a dedicated fundraiser or by investing in events or major donor cultivation. By Years 4 and 5, while the return on investment has fallen, the extra input appears to be paying off handsomely in absolute terms.

Year	Donors	New donors	Lapsed Donors	Repeat donors
1	95	79	n/a	n/a
2	189	151	57	38
3	240	150	99	90
4	333	223	130	110
5	370	227	190	143

Table 10 Annual Campaign Effectiveness: Donor Numbers

This table also helps uncover interesting and often surprising trends. For instance, in this example, while the number of donors giving goes up in a steady way, this does not give the whole picture. For instance, look at the number of lapsed donors. More often than not, they are going up at a higher percentage rate than overall donor numbers. Putting greater focus on lapsed donors would be a very good idea for this school in the following year!

Year	Gift Size (£)					
	0-100	101-999	1,000-4,999	5,0000-9,999	10,000+	Average
1	92	2	1	0	0	£85
2	185	2	2	0	0	£79
3	230	5	2	2	0	£143
4	304	17	7	4	2	£268
5	322	26	11	7	4	£399

Table 11 Annual Campaign Effectiveness: Gift Sizes

By plotting this table, you ensure that you are focused on increasing the average size of your donations. This is important because you will never be very effective if you only focus on small gifts. So in this table, it can be seen that Year 2 led to a dip in average donations – not particularly good, unless there was a strong push to gain new donors, who often give low amounts at the start. Conversely, by Years 4 and 5, some larger donations are coming in, probably from formal applications or because several major donors have been cultivated. This school is going in the right direction!

If you really want to make the most of trends, then look to benchmark yourself with a similar type of school to assess your performance. While your numbers might look good in their own right, by comparing them with others you might spot new trends and techniques that will guide future direction. For instance, if your neighbouring school is having huge success with trusts and foundations then you probably want to do something similar.

- **Maintaining momentum**
  Once you have successfully undertaken one Annual Campaign, it is relatively straightforward to keep up the momentum, simply changing the theme from year to year. You can then safely rely on a certain amount of additional annual income to help your school develop. If your first campaign has been a little underwhelming or chaotic do not give up unless you have very good reason. It is not uncommon for this to be the case first time. The important thing is to learn from any mistakes and try and improve on the numbers.

Capital Campaigns
i. Purpose
As the name implies the Capital Campaign has one main aim: providing funds for a capital project.

Generally speaking, a Capital Campaign that aims to raise five times the amount of your Annual Campaign is realistic but greater sums are possible if there is a clear need. Either way, it is a major undertaking and requires much more focus and effort than an Annual Campaign.

ii. Content
The execution of the Capital Campaign is similar to that of an Annual Campaign, except that there are additional stages where you check the

feasibility and viability of the Capital Campaign. This gives five stages instead of three:

1. Internal readiness
2. Case Statement
3. External evaluation
4. Marketing plan
5. Implementation and monitoring

A word of warning! – When undertaking a Capital Campaign, you are effectively asking your donors to dig especially deeply for a one-off, special project. As a result, it will likely negatively impact on your Annual Campaign and also lead to a drop-off in income once the Campaign has finished as donors will feel that they have front-ended their giving.

Of course, you might not consider that a problem if your involvement with the school will end in a year or two! However, in the long term interests of the school, you will need to weigh up whether it is worth a Capital Campaign largely monopolising your efforts over its lifetime.

Internal readiness

A number of factors need to be in place before embarking in earnest on a Capital Campaign:

- The commitment and involvement of senior leaders of the school. For instance, a successful campaign is very unlikely without the head teacher and the chair of governors taking an active role.

- The ability and readiness of major donors to give substantial sums towards the campaign goal. If this is not the case, for example if the school is new to fundraising, then concentrating on smaller Annual Campaigns to build up a group of prospects and donors is advisable.

The above factors are essential but other elements should also be considered including:

- Time and resource available for fundraising
- Competent staff who understand the campaign process
- The size and position of the school in relation to its campaign goals

- The state of the economy
- Local issues pertinent to the campaign.

Case Statement

Once you have decided that you are ready to undertake a Capital Campaign, you will need to produce the document that makes the arguments for support. As with the Annual Campaign, this Case Statement is taken from the Case for Support (page 88) and should show:

- The organisation and what it is about
- Why the campaign is needed
- What difference the capital build will make
- Benefits to donors in participating
- The financial needs.

As you will almost certainly be raising a larger sum than the Annual Campaign, you might consider spending more time and money on the document – you will want to ensure that it sets the right tone!

External evaluation

Once you have written the Case Statement, you are in a position to gain feedback on its strengths and weaknesses. By asking external funders and stakeholders to assess the aims and priorities of your campaign you will ensure that your ambitions are realistic – much better to do this now than find out half way through that you have been over optimistic.

Evaluators

Those who would make worthy assessors include:

- Those who are supportive of the school
- Those who have given financial support (or might do so)
- Any fundraisers who have made a significant contribution
- Anybody who might become actively engaged in the campaign (or whom you would like to do so).

As well as providing an outsider's view of your plans, this stage can also unlock potential future support because you can ask innocuous questions like, 'Would you support this campaign?' This is a less intrusive way of asking someone to give than making approaches when the campaign parameters are already decided. It is also easier for the fundraiser making the asks!

The ideal means of undertaking such assessments is face-to-face with your representative being objective and not too wedded to the plans – you want to be able to hear any negative comments without being defensive. This is why professional, external fundraisers are often used at this point. However, budgets vary and if yours is limited you might wish to mail a questionnaire to potential assessors.

Items to assess

Items you are trying to assess at this stage include:

- Are the school's needs accurate?
- Are the size and number of big donations you are expecting realistic?
- Is it the right time to undertake a Capital Campaign?
- Are there external opportunities available?
- Would the external assessor be interested in being involved in some way, for instance as a fundraiser or opening doors to others?
- Does the assessor know any individuals or organisations that would make a contribution of £10,000? (Modify the figure in relation to your school's reach, size and goals.)

Final campaign proposition

Having undertaken the previous stages, you will now have a much clearer idea of what is feasible and what is not – you have avoided the most common mistake which is simply to launch a campaign and hope for the best!

Your Case Statement should be updated with the intelligence you have received. For instance, if parts of your plans have not been well-received then you can take them out of the document, altering the budget accordingly. Similarly if nobody thinks your £1m target is achievable then you might need to scale back your plans. Conversely, you might have opened up various funding routes which mean that you can include more elements or indeed upgrade your plans.

Unless feedback on your campaign has been extremely negative, your reworked Case Statement will be ready to use. In addition, you should have identified a number of funding opportunities and even unlocked some support.

Bear in mind that unless you have raised 30-50% of the goal, you should be wary about announcing your aims publicly. Only if you are very confident that you can meet the target should you go public. Instead, if there is a shortfall, you should be seeking major gifts and building a group of volunteers and supporters before going to all parents and wider afield.

Marketing plan

The marketing plan can be drawn up following the process outlined for the Annual Campaign (page 132) with a few slight amendments.

Firstly, you will need more face-to-face meetings because you are asking for higher amounts of support. Consequently, you will need to ensure that the head teacher, chair of governors and other senior representatives of the school are prepared to put in considerably more work than for the Annual Campaign. This critical point is worth checking from the outset – a surprising number of schools, both state and independent, have run into trouble when the head teacher proves elusive and not fully engaged.

Secondly, as mentioned above, it is a good idea to have raised a considerable amount of the target before you officially launch your campaign. As part of this endeavour, it is worth seeking a big donation to launch the campaign. This will inspire others to give and removes any scepticism about raising very large sums. It will be even more effective if you incorporate a match-challenge with this donation.

Thirdly, you will need to spend more on your marketing so, for instance, your Case Statement and supporting documentation should be produced to a very high standard.

Fourthly, you should seriously consider putting together a Campaign Board. This can be made up of senior staff as well as major donors and volunteers offering particular skills, such as marketing. You will want this group to open their networks so that more donors are found, particularly larger ones. They should also be able to offer advice when times prove difficult or the campaign appears somewhat stalled, which inevitably will happen. Above all, ensure that this group is willing to work for the campaign – the worst thing that you can have is a group of people all ready to offer advice but never willing to get their hands dirty themselves.

Fifthly, as the campaign will take time you should plan various activities to inject renewed vigour through its course. There is a tendency for enthusiasm to wane at various points so good marketing techniques will prevent this happening. For instance, you might plan an extra special event or you might hold back a match-challenge for later in the campaign.

15. Campaigns – bringing it all together

Implementation and monitoring

Monitoring of a Capital Campaign is largely about ensuring milestones are met and the campaign is on track. So your Campaign Director must be someone who is good at project management, amongst other things. Meeting regularly, such as monthly, will allow the Campaign Board to keep on top of progress and take remedial action wherever needed.

Regular reports to key stakeholders, such as major donors, will keep them informed of progress as well. This keeps these stakeholders engaged and, if you are falling behind, they can also provide an external boost to fundraising totals.

Celebration

Of course, do not forget to celebrate once your campaign has finished. While there will no doubt be a sense of achievement, you will probably have exhausted most of your fundraising community. So thank them properly, perhaps with a large party – once you have given a little time for people to recover, you will want to suggest your next campaign!

Endowments

An endowment is a sum of money (the principal) which provides an income to a school from the interest earned on that sum. This money is traditionally used to fund ongoing costs that normal fundraising doesn't typically cover. They have been popular with higher education but not so much with secondary or primary education, largely because other areas of fundraising are easier and more cost-effective than raising funds for endowments.

i. Pre-campaign checklist

Factors to have in place before embarking on an Endowment Fund Campaign include:

- You already have a successful fundraising programme, which will not be severely impacted by this new development
- You have a committed governing body that is aware of the difficulties and time required for this type of fundraising
- You have a means of investing the funds raised
- Your school/project will exist for a minimum of several years
- You are prepared to put time and effort into a fundraising vehicle which might not elicit funds for some time, even years

- You have run through the feasibility of an Endowment Fund with your biggest funders and should have a clear idea of where at least 30% of your initial target is going to come from.

ii. Scope
Once you feel you are ready to embark on setting up an endowment, you should consider the following questions:

- Do you want your endowment to serve a certain purpose or be unrestricted in its use? The latter type has more flexibility but fundraising is generally harder for this purpose.
- Do you want your endowment to go on indefinitely or only for a finite amount of time? The advantage of the latter is that you can use the principal at the end of the term to fund a capital project.

iii. Legal constitution
You will need a lawyer to set up the original endowment, and at least one trustee to manage it. The trustee should also have policies that make clear:

- What funds can be accepted (e.g. can shares be included?)
- How the funds should be invested
- How the interest (and principal, if applicabl should be spent
- How donors should be updated.

iv. Fundraising for an Endowment Fund
Follow the process for fundraising as per the Capital Campaign on pages 138 to 143. Bear in mind that while endowment funds are highly beneficial they are perhaps the most difficult to fundraise for – it is simply much harder to get funders enthused about what is essentially an investment vehicle in comparison to something immediately tangible like a sports hall. However, if you are successfully building an endowment fund then you know that your fundraising is going very well!

15. Campaigns – bringing it all together

Chapter 15 in a nutshell

In this final chapter, drawing on the advice given in earlier chapters, the advanced fundraising techniques required to run Annual, Capital and Endowment Fund Campaigns are described.

16
SUMMARY

Fundraising is very much an art. A book such as this can only show you the principles and it will be up to you to fit them to your needs, circumstances and personal make-up. Indeed, the manner with which you go about raising support will be different to mine, just as the dynamics of friendship differ between people.

Having said that, whatever your level of fundraising, if you can adopt a few of the suggestions in this book you should raise your performance quite considerably. Those undertaking a more methodical approach, such as the suggested roll-out of fundraising activities in Chapter 5, could see six, possibly seven, figure annual income levels reached. In addition, the services and products listed in the Resources section will almost certainly help, either by easing your workload or by improving your fundraising effectiveness.

In the 1990s, higher education witnessed a step change in its approach to fundraising and one would hope, particularly with squeezes on school budgets, that such a transformation is under way in primary and secondary education. This book gives you the tools to succeed, if accompanied by plenty of effort and determination. I will therefore sign off by wishing you the very best in your fundraising endeavours. Anybody who has done even a modicum of serious fundraising knows that practitioners often fluctuate between great highs and terrible lows as funding decisions are made (it is not for the faint-hearted!) So if you are new to the field or an old hand all too familiar with its workings, I wish you well and hope this book creates a few more highs for you. Good luck!

17
RESOURCES

Directories of funders
Trusts and Foundations
- Charity Commission for England and Wales – the online register of the charity regulator allows free search of all registered charities which, though time-consuming, can be useful for identifying local grant-makers: (apps.charitycommission.gov.uk/showcharity/registerof charities/RegisterHomePage.aspx)
- For the Scottish Charity Regulator, see: www.oscr.org.uk/, and for the Charity Commission for Northern Ireland: www.charitycommissionni.org.uk/

Most fundraisers from trusts, however, will want to invest in one or more of these paid listings services:

- Trustfunding.org.uk: the Directory of Social Change's directory of trusts and foundations (www.trustfunding.org.uk)
- Schools Funding Network – provides a monthly list of upcoming grants to school members (www.schoolsfundingnetwork.co.uk)
- Grants 4 Schools – provides details of the big funders and sends regular emails (www.grants4schools.info)
- Newcharities.org – provides reports on newly registered charities (www.newcharities.org)
- Social Partnership Marketing – publishes Invisible Grantmakers, an annual report of trusts not featured in other directories (www socialpartnershipmarketing.co.uk).

Companies
- Yell is a good guide for finding local businesses (www.yell.com)
- Companygiving.org.uk provides giving details of approximately 500 companies (www.companygiving.org.uk)
- Companies House – gives access to free and subscription based services (www.companieshouse.gov.uk)
- London Stock Exchange – gives detailed information on all quoted UK and international companies (www.londonstockexchange com). A spreadsheet of all London Stock Exchange listed companies

can be downloaded from: www.londonstockexchange.com/statistics/companies-and-issuers/companies-and-issuers.htm

Statutory Funds
- Education Funding Agency – gives details of general government funding to schools (www.gov.uk/government/organisations education-funding-agency)
- Governmentfunding.co.uk – provides details of a range of local, regional and national government grants (www.governmentfunding org.uk)

Livery Companies
- www.liverycompanies.com – provides a complete list of livery companies of the City of London, with the names of the current Master and Clerk and links to individual company websites (www liverycompanies.com/)
- Livery Schoools Link – links schools with livery companies (www.liveryschoolslink.co.uk/)

Other fundraising resources
Crowdfunding
- Crowdfunding: the wisdom and wallets of crowds – offers a useful and free introduction to crowdfunding. www.nominettrust.org.uk/knowledge-centre/publications/spring-giving-insight/report-crowdfunding-wisdom-and-wallets-crowds

Charity Commission for England and Wales
- The Charity Commission document Charity fundraising: a guide to trustee duties (CC20) gives an overview of good fundraising practice and current legislation. See: www.gov.uk/government/publications/charities-and-fundraising-cc20

Databases
- Blackbaud provides highly sophisticated fundraising databases. Costs can however be high. (www.blackbaud.co.uk/notforprofit schools)
- thankQ is a very popular database, one version of which is focused on educational establishments. Price depends on features required. www.theaccessgroup.com/crm-nfp/

- Salesforce is a similarly good choice. You can apply for free usage, saving you significant costs. (www.salesforce.org/nonprofit/fundraise/)
- IT for Charities gives a list of fundraising databases: (www.itforcharities.co.uk/database-software/fundraising-software/)

Digital platforms
- JustGiving is the UK's biggest general fundraising platform (www.justgiving.com)
- Schools Funding Network is a dedicated fundraising platform for schools, also offering a Gift Aid administration service (www.schoolsfundingnetwork.co.uk)

Fundraising Regulator
- The Fundraising Regulator holds the Code of Fundraising Practice for the UK, and aims 'to ensure that fundraising is respectful, open, honest and accountable to the public'. See www.fundraisingregulator.org.uk. Further information on fundraising regulation in Scotland and Northern Ireland is given at www.fundraisingregulator.org.uk/about/regulation-in-scotland-and-northern-ireland/

General fundraising ideas
- Easy Fundraising is a free service where you can shop with your favourite online stores and at no extra cost raise funds for your good cause (www.easyfundraising.org.uk/ideas/fundraising-ideas-for-schools/)
- Sofii: Showcase of fundraising innovation and inspiration (www.sofii.org/)
- UK Fundraising: the UK's first stop for digital fundraising and other fundraising resources (www.fundraising.co.uk)

Gift Aid
- General Gift Aid guidance from HMRC is given at www.gov.uk/claim-gift-aid. However for schools not registered as charities, www.schoolsfundingnetwork.co.uk/how-it-works/gift-aid recovery-scheme covers all your Gift Aid requirements immediately, without the need to register with HMRC.

Legacy fundraising
- Will Aid offers an annual opportunity to make a Will with a donation to the cause of your choice in lieu of the solicitor's fee (www.willaid.org.uk)

Payroll Giving
- A list of HMRC-approved Payroll Giving agencies can be found at: www.gov.uk/government/publications/payroll-giving-approved-agencies/list-of-approved-payroll-giving-agencies

PTA support
- PTA UK offers a variety of resources that help schools and PTAs work together. They also offer a very good insurance product for events. (www.pta.org.uk)

Text giving
- JustTextGiving allows you to receive donations by text at no cost. The service is a partnership between Vodafone and JustGiving (www justtextgiving.co.uk)

Wealth screening
Companies that offer wealth screening services include:
- Factary (www.factary.com)
- Milestone Research (www.milestoneresearch.co.uk)
- Prospecting for Gold (www.prospectingforgold.co.uk/wealth)

Bibliography
Fundraising disciplines
Achieving Excellence in Fund Raising by Henry A Rosso & Associates (Jossey Bass, 2nd Edition 2003)
Annual Giving Primer: How to Boost Annual Giving Results by Scott C Stevenson, Ed. (Jossey-Bass, 2013)
Capital Campaigns by Trudy Hayden (Directory of Social Change, 2006)
Conducting A Successful Annual Giving Program by Kent E Dove, Jeffrey A Lindauer, Carolyn P Madvig (Wiley, 2001)
Conducting A Successful Capital Campaign by Kent E Dove (Wiley, 2010)
Conducting A Successful Major Gifts & Planned Giving Program: A Comprehensive Guide and Resource by Kent E Dove, Alan M Spears, Thomas W Herbert (Wiley, 2013)

Legacy Fundraising: The Art of Seeking Bequests by Sebastian Wilberforce (Directory of Social Change, 2010)
Legacy Fundraising from Scratch by Simon George (spmfundessentials, 2011)
Major Donor Fundraising by Margaret M Holman & Lucy Sargent (Directory of Social Change, 2006)
Major Donors – Finding Big Gifts in Your Database & Online by Ted Hart, James M Greenfield, Pamela M Gignac and Christopher Carnie (Wiley, 2006)
The 11 Questions Every Donor Asks and the Answers All Donors Crave: How You Can Inspire Someone to Give Generously by Harvey McKinnon (Emerson & Church, 2008)
The Fundraiser Who Wanted More: The 5 Laws of Persuasion that Transform your Results by Rob Woods (Woods Training Limited, 2015)
The Guide to Educational Grants 2016/17 by Jodie Huyton and Gabriele Zagnojute (Directory of Social Change, 2016)
Volunteering – The Business Case: The Benefits of Corporate Volunteering Programmes in Education (Corporate Citizenship, 2010)

Prospect research
Prospect Research for Fundraisers: The Essential Handbook by Jennifer J Filla and Helen E Brown (Wiley, 2013)
Prospect Research: A Primer for Growing Nonprofits by Cecilia Hogan (Jones and Bartlett, 2007)
Prospect Research by Robin Jones and Rebecca Funnell (spmfundessentials, 2011)

General
Best Practice Benchmarking: A Management Guide by Sylvia Codling (2nd Revised Edition, Gower Publishing Limited, 1995)
Clarity and Impact: Inform and Impress with Your Reports and Talks by Jon Moon (Oberon Publishing Limited, 2016)
Closing Techniques (That Really Work!) by Stephan Schiffman (Adams Media Corp, 1994)
Everything is Negotiable: How to Get the Best Deal Every Time by Gavin Kennedy (4th Revised Edition, Random House Business, 2008)
Harvard Business Essentials: Power, Influence and Persuasion: Sell Your Ideas and Make Things Happen (Harvard Business Review, 2005)
How Not To Come Second: The Art of Winning Business Pitches by David Kean (Cyan Communications, 2006)
Influence: The Psychology of Persuasion by Robert B Cialdini, PhD (Revised

Edition, Harper Business, 2007)
Richer Lives: Why Rich People Give by Theresa Lloyd and Beth Breeze (Directory of Social Change, 2013)
Social Media for Social Good: A How-to Guide for Nonprofits by Heather Mansfield (McGraw-Hill Education, 2011)
The Gift Aid Guide: Rules Relating to Charity Donations by Individuals by Graham Elliott (spmfundessentials, 2013).

ABOUT THE AUTHOR

Nick Ryan is a development professional with a broad range of fundraising experience in both the charity and education sectors, having raised tens of millions of pounds of non-statutory funds and hundreds of millions of pounds of statutory income for good causes.

The founder and director of organisational development consultancy Vantage Fundraising (www.vantagefundraising.co.uk), Nick was also instrumental in founding Schools Funding Network (www.schoolsfundingnetwork.co.uk), which enables educational establishments to fundraise for any project, large or small, and to interact with major donors, charitable trusts, foundations, parents and other potential funders. The service, which Nick still runs on behalf of the charity The Funding Exchange, presently involves hundreds of schools and major donors across England and Wales.

Nick lives in North London with his wife, Meg, and two children, Ben and Lucy. When not helping organisations to grow and raise funds, he can often be found running in his local Park Run or cultivating his allotment, both for food and as a haven for wildlife. His long-term aim is to be able to speak a number of languages very well, rather than several very badly.

INDEX

30-second pitch, 93-94
    producing your pitch, 93-94
    purpose, 93

annual campaigns, 132-144
    calendar of activities, 135
    Case Statement, 133
    content, 132-133
    gift tables, 133-134
    implementation and monitoring, 136-138
    leverage, 135
    long-term trends, 136-138
    maintaining momentum, 138
    marketing plan, 133-135
    purpose, 132
    targeting, 134
activities, 19-25
    prioritising, 25
affinity motivation, 32, 37, 40, 69, 117, 123
Age UK, 63
alumni, 29, 37, 66, 79
    approach, 39
    motivation, 10
    overcoming engagement difficulties, 10
    types of fundraising activity, 10
approach
    generic groups, 36-37
    impact, 40
    timing, 41
    types, 37
Aweber (www.aweber.com), 47

bit.ly, 104
blogs, 99
Bursar/business manager, 40
    motivation for fundraising, 9
    overcoming engagement difficulties, 9
    types of fundraising activity, 9
businesses
    guides, 30
    local, 30, 33, 37
    national, 30, 33
    owned by ex-pupils, 30
    owned by parents, 30
    where parents work, 30

Campaign Board, 142
Cancer Research, 63
capacity, 3
    increasing, 4
capital campaigns, 138-143
    Case Statement, 140
    content, 138-143
    external evaluation, 140-142
    implementation and monitoring, 143
    internal readiness, 139-140
    marketing plan, 142
    purpose, 138
Case for Support, 14, 88-90
    current objectives, 88-89
    essential content, 88-89
    future direction, 88
    means of giving, 89
    plan of action, 89
cash, 13-14
    from companies, 74

Cause-related marketing (CRM), 24-25, 30, 74, 83-86
    ethical guidance, 85
    how to broker, 84
    local businesses, 83
    pricing, 84-85
choosing your project, 13-14
Cialdini, Robert B, 109
community fundraising, 20, 29, 30, 51-52
    inspiring volunteers, 51-52
    secondary activities, 52
    sponsored activities, 52
types of activity, 51
Companies House, 68
Companygiving.org.uk, 30
company fundraising, 4, 22-23, 29, 30, 73-76
    cash donations, 74
    cause-related marketing (CRM), 74
    how much to ask for, 75
    in-kind support, 74
    marketing budget, 75
    philanthropic budget, 75
    proposal, 74
    staff time, 74
    why companies give, 73
Corporate Social Responsibility, 30
crowdfunding, 96-97
    definition, 96
    running a campaign, 96

data capture, 54-55
data protection, 48, 126
database, 29, 67
donors, 4
    keeping them engaged, 126-128
    motivations, 31-34, 40, 123
    potential, 29-31
    VIP, 7, 29, 54

endowments, 143-144
    Endowment Fund, 144
    legacies, 82-83, 89
    legal constitution, 144
    pre-campaign checklist, 143
    scope, 144
ethical considerations, 27-29, 33, 85
event fundraising, 20, 29, 30, 38, 53-56
    co-ordinator, 54
    measurements, 55
    post-event, 55-56
    pre-event objectives, 53
    tasks, 53-54

Facebook, 29, 97, 98, 99, 100-102
    content, 101-102
    events, 102
    getting started, 100-101
    groups, 102
    increasing your community, 102
financial checks, 28, 124
Flickr, 99, 100

GetResponse (www.getresponse.com), 47
Gift Aid, 9, 49, 52, 55, 72, 92-93, 96, 135
    claiming, 93
    Gift Aid Recovery System, 92
gift-in-kind donations, 85

Google, 30, 50, 68, 99
Google Analytics, 50, 51, 99
Google Images, 100
Government funding, 31
governors, 29, 36, 66, 85
    motivation for fundraising, 8
    overcoming engagement difficulties, 8
    types of fundraising activity, 8

head teacher, 40, 53, 142
    motivation for fundraising, 7
    overcoming engagement difficulties, 7
    types of fundraising activity, 7
Helping Out: A national survey of volunteering and charitable giving (Cabinet Office, 2007), 15
Hootsuite, 100, 104

In-kind support, 74
    asking for, 17
    why funders give, 16-17
Influence, Robert B Cialdini, 109
Information Commissioner's Office (ICO), 48-49
Instagiv, 79

JustGiving, 49, 52, 93
JustTextGiving, 79

legacies, 24, 29, 80-83
    benchmarking, 83
    marketing, 81-83
    measurements, 83
    pecuniary, 80
    publicity vehicles, 82
    residual, 80
    updates, 83
    who to target, 82
LinkedIn, 29, 68, 99
Livery companies, 30
    approach, 39

MailChimp (mailchimp.com), 47, 49
major donor fundraising, 4, 22, 29, 45, 65-73
    amount, 71
    approach, 36, 65-73
    giving capacity, 68
    identification, 65-66
    interest, 68-69
    measurement and review, 73
    objections, 71
    plan, 69-70
    prospect list, 43
    research, 67-69
    thanking, 72-73
    timing, 70, 71, 72
    wealth screening, 67

match-giving, 85, 94-95
    challenges, 95
memorandum of understanding (MoU), 79
mutual benefit motivation, 25, 33, 40, 69, 75, 117, 123

National Audit Office, 92
networking, 29, 108-109
    body language, 108
    goals, 108
    post-event, 109
    pre-networking activities, 108
newsletter, 19, 29, 30, 31, 45-49
    content, 46-47
    distribution, 47
    e-newsletter, 47-48, 98, 100, 104
    photographs, 48-49
    purpose, 45-46
    style, 46
NSPCC, 48

Ofsted, 7, 8
one-off donations, 85

parents, 29, 37, 66
    approach, 39
    motivation for fundraising, 8
    overcoming engagement difficulties, 8
    types of fundraising activity, 8
Payroll Giving, 22, 52, 63-65, 85
    costs, 64
    how to set up, 64
    leveraging donations, 65
    Payroll Giving Agency, 64
Peer-to-peer giving, 40
philanthropic motivation, 32, 40, 69, 117, 123, 124
policy
    acceptance, 27, 123, 135
    ethical, 27-28, 89
    social media, 100
professional fundraiser
    motivation for fundraising, 11
    overcoming engagement difficulties, 11
    types of fundraising activity, 10
psychology of influence, 109-111
    principles, 109-111
PTA, 85
PTA UK, 52
pupils, 4
    motivation for fundraising, 10
    overcoming engagement difficulties, 10
    types of fundraising activity, 9

raffles and lotteries, 21, 29, 30, 38, 52, 60-62
    Gambling Commission, 61
    Licences and regulations, 60-61
    local licensing authority, 61
    marketing, 62
    prizes, 60
    tickets, 60
recognition
    table, 123
recycling as a fundraiser, 21, 29, 30, 62-63
    recycling for charities, 63
    what can be recycled, 62
religious motivation, 32
Rotary Clubs, 30, 31
RSPB, 16

School Hire, 77
School Plus, 77
school premises, 76-77
    contracts, 77
    exploiting, 23, 76-77
    marketing, 76-77
    outsourcing, 77
    what can be hired out, 76
Schools Funding Network, 49, 52, 64, 79, 92
social media, 29, 38, 41, 49, 97-104
    objectives, 99
    overview, 97-98
    strategy, 98-99
    tips, 99
social motivation, 34, 40, 69, 117, 123

sponsorship, 23-24, 31, 77-79, 85
    contracts, 79
    how much to charge, 78
    what can be sponsored, 77
staff
    motivation for fundraising, 9
    overcoming engagement difficulties, 9
    types of fundraising activity, 9
    volunteering, 85
Stewardship Programme, 126-130
    database, 126
    end of year reports, 128-129
    keeping donors engaged, 126-128
    segmentation, 128
    who goes in, 126
storytelling, 106-107
    anonymity, 107
    embellishments, 107
    why stories work, 107
Sunday Times Rich List, 29

Text giving, 24, 29, 79-80
    fundraising by text, 79
    monitoring, 80
    providers, 79
The Funding Exchange, 92
The Guide to UK Company Giving (DSC), 30, 31
time factors, 40
Times Educational Supplement, 1
timetable of activities, 41-42
Trust and statutory applications, 20, 30-31, 38
    approach, 39, 41
    eligibility, 56
    following up, 60
    local, 30
    national, 30
    structure, 56-59
Trustfunding.org.uk, 31
Twitter, 97, 98, 99, 103-104
    content, 104
    hashtags, 103
    privacy, 103
    retweeting, 103
    segmentation, 103
    sign up, 103
    timings, 104
    Twitdom, 104
    Twtpoll, 104

volunteers, 3, 53
    attracting, 15-16
    managing, 16

Walker, Dr Catherine, 94
website, 19, 29, 30, 89, 98, 50-51
    content, 49
    essential information, 49
    giving amounts, 51
    measurement, 50-51
    Search Engine Optimisation, 50
    video, 50
Woodland Trust, 63
YouTube, 99

Zoopla, 67

The Charity First Series

For the full list of titles in the Charity First Series, including titles in preparation, see www.charityfirstseries.org.

Titles already published include:
Effective Media Relations for Charities – What journalists want and how to deliver it
Academy Schools – from Conversion to Successful Operation
Beyond the Collection Plate - Developing Church Income from Different Sources
Effective Media Relations for Charities
Fundraising for Small Charities
Legacy Fundraising from Scratch
Major Gift Fundraising
Organising and Operating a US Charity
Prospect Research
Raising Funds from Grant Makers
Structuring Not-for-Profit Operations in the UK
The Gift Aid Guide

Also published by Social Partnership Marketing
Invisible Grantmakers - an annual listing of unpublished grantmaking trusts.
See www.socialpartnershipmarketing.co.uk for further details.